AF244164

BLESSED

IN THE

DARKNESS

S.J RYE

This is an IndieMosh book

brought to you by MoshPit Publishing, an imprint of
Mosher's Business Support Pty Ltd

PO Box 147

Hazelbrook NSW 2779

indiemosh.com.au

Cataloguing-in-Publication entry is available from the National Library of Australia: http://catalogue.nla.gov.au/

Title:	Blessed in the Darkness
Author:	Rye, Stacey (1996–)
ISBNs:	978-1-925595-02-4 (paperback)
	978-1-925529-91-3 (ebook – epub)
	978-1-925529-92-0 (ebook – mobi)

This is a memoir based on the author's recollection of names, places, events, conversations and other details. Not all items in the author's memory have been included and some may have been omitted, compressed, combined or changed for expediency, to protect the privacy of others or because this is the way the author remembers them. While you may think you recognise certain characters, events or places in this story, it is most likely that this will be by coincidence only.

Cover artwork & design by Dylan Proctor and James Brewer

Book Layout ©2015 BookDesignTemplates.com

Contents

To my tree
Thanks for believing
xo

I sat thinking about all that had happened and felt defeated.

How could I let such a precious thing slip from my hands?

Beaten and bruised, it wasn't only my skin showing signs of the years.

I love you and I know you love me, too.

Sometimes people aren't supposed to be together;

Sometimes people just don't know how to love in the right way.

Introduction

The following story you are about to read is not just words spilled across a page. It is more than consonants and vowels, paragraphs and chapters... more than a compilation of phrases to create a literary art piece. What you are about to read is real, raw and honest. It is my life! When I first started writing this book, I didn't realize how colossal a task it was going to be. I assumed scribing what has already taken place would be simple.

Oh how wrong I was!

I had to dredge up dark times I would rather have forgotten altogether. To accurately capture my thoughts and feelings during those times, I had to slip back into the shoes of my past-self. It would have been a heck of a lot easier to write from a place of victory — from where I am today. However, I was determined to capture the true essence of what it's really like for a young life to transform. Because of this approach, and my commitment to being as authentic as possible, *this book contains swearing.*

My intention is not to offend or upset any readers. Instead, I have included these words because that was who I was at the time. If I were to dilute my honest thoughts and language, I would incorrectly represent the journey I have travelled. I pray as you read this book, you will be able to understand the mind of a lost, broken and confused young person. I also pray this book brings light and hope to those who find themselves in similar situations. I truly understand how you feel (trust me, you're about to read all about it!). I pray you read this book with an open heart and become inspired to make steps toward a happier, healthier life.

If God can radically change my life, He can definitely do the same for you!

I lumbered up the ramp to the front door, knowing my entire life was going to completely change. I desperately wanted to run straight back to the familiar embrace of what I was fleeing. I hesitated, questioning if this was the right thing to do. Guilt spread over me like wildfire. I was hazy and irritable from all the vodka I had consumed the night before. I glanced back at my friends in the car, feeling so thankful they were there with me, even though I was embarrassed by them seeing me like this.

A tall, bald, lanky man opened the door.

"Hey. Umm, I'm Stacey. Melinda called you guys about me?"

This is it! There's no turning back now.

I realized he was the one Melinda had spoken to earlier that week and felt relieved he already knew who I was. I really didn't want to explain my life story to some stranger... on some random doorstep... whilst nursing a terrible hangover.

He introduced himself as Ian, and helped me gather my bags from the car. He was a remarkably cheerful guy and doing his best to make me feel welcome. I was attempting to appear sober as we entered his office, and I slouched into the couch across from him. He could probably still smell the sweet scent of regret from last night.

He was asking me questions... while I focused on making sense:

"Seventeen..."

"Since last year..."

"One..."

"Yeah, sometimes..."

"No..."

"I'm not really sure anymore, maybe..."
"Yes..."
"No..."
"Brother..."

My heart was racing faster with every question.

Why couldn't he just pull my file from those countless doctor's appointments and therapy sessions?

Ian explained the rules of the house and briefed me on my rights as a resident. He had me sign an Agreement, and then we made casual chit chat. This was probably his strategy to calm me down.

"You seem like a good kid, Stacey. I know you're going to be fine. And I know that the big man has it all sorted."

Wait... what?! Big man? God?! What the hell does God have to do with this?! Is that even who he is talking about? Probably... he does seem like a weird Christian.

He showed me to my room and took me for a tour of the rest of the house. There was only one other resident currently checked in. She was sitting in the living room on her phone. She looked older and a lot tougher than me. I felt intimidated. Her name was Claire[1], and it turns out she was two years younger than me. Everything within me hoped that we could get along. I was feeling absolutely terrified – a new environment with different people and new boundaries and routines... making enemies was

---

1   Names of (all) residents have been changed to protect the privacy of individuals

the worst thing I could do. First impressions were going to make or break me in here.

Ian interrupted my thoughts with another rule.
"Residents aren't allowed to open the door..."
We had moved toward the kitchen when there was a sudden knock at the door. Claire was peering out the window trying to work out who it was.
I already knew.

"Shit. It's my therapist..."

I can spot Melinda from a mile away. She is tall, with gorgeous long red hair, and her smile invites calm to the restless heart. She consistently shines positivity... but not in the bullshit way that makes you want to throw up. I followed Ian to the door and watched as her face changed when she saw me standing there. It was strange to see her outside her office. This had happened once before at the supermarket, but I totally avoided her. It's like when you see teachers outside of school. It's super awkward and you can't believe they actually have a life that doesn't involve sitting in a classroom. That's what it was like with Melinda. I had spent many hours sitting in her office, confessing my deepest, darkest secrets... seeing her outside that context was just bizarre.

"Oh darling! I wasn't planning on seeing you here so soon!"

I began tearing up.

This is all so foreign.

I felt completely vulnerable. I didn't know who Ian was. I didn't know why Claire was here. The whole house had a juvenile detention vibe. I felt utterly lost and now here was Melinda... the one thing I knew. Her eagerness to comfort me only seemed to make me more upset. With no idea what was going to happen to me, I just wanted to walk out the door and disappear. I didn't want to face reality. Melinda had come to discuss some things with Ian, so she planned an appointment with me for the following day. Still dazed, I found my way back to the living room and sat across from Claire. We were silent until Melinda and Ian came out of the office.

"I'll see you tomorrow afternoon, sweetheart."

Please don't go, Mel. Please don't leave me here.

CHAPTER TWO

Ironically, Claire and I ended up bonding over tea. Ordinarily, the residents follow a roster for house chores and cooking dinner but because it was the first night for both of us, Ian offered to cook for the night. Claire told me how she had spent time in several other youth shelters, which was oddly comforting. Knowing that she understood the ins-and-outs somehow calmed me. We questioned Ian about his life and discovered he was a Christian... as I assumed. I was glad there was an opportunity to keep asking questions over our meal because it distracted me from the food on my plate. I also hoped it was diverting Ian and Claire from how anxious I was becoming.

I helped Ian wash up after we ate while asking more questions. If he was going to pry into my life (even if it was his job!) I wanted to know who he was and what his deal was. It turns out, he was a super cool guy and not at all like the other Christians I know. This intrigued me. Claire had left, so I continued to hang out with Ian in the lounge room. When Melinda had first told me about the shelter, I googled profusely... searching for every bit of information I could find. After a lead up of several months, it felt surreal to finally be here! The security screens on the windows made me feel particularly uncomfortable... I had never been in a house that looked so much like a prison. The lounge room however, looked like a normal home and the entertainment was decent! A pool table took up almost one side of the room and there were several puzzles and games in a cupboard. The couch was like an oasis. When I was sitting on it, I couldn't really see any of the health and lifestyle posters that were taped randomly to the walls. It was as if, for just a moment, we forgot where we were and what was really going on.

I had chosen the bed that was in the same position as the one at my parents' house — along the left wall, with a bedside table on the right. I was hoping this would make it easier to settle at night. There was an unusual sky-light window above me. The moon hung in its centre, perfectly framed. There were three beds in each bedroom and Claire had the one furthest from me. Hopefully she wouldn't hear me crying as much.

I tossed and turned until the moon rose out of sight. My mind was overthrown by thoughts of the unknown. I was so distressed and I had no idea how to process what had happened. I wished I could fall asleep and wake to this being a terrible dream. I wanted to open my eyes and for all of this to be some kind of horrible nightmare that would be no longer the second I open my eyes. I curled in a ball and faced the wall.

Please let this all be a dream. Please, please, please.

I had no idea what was going to happen to me... no idea at all.

I woke early to a boat horn as it sailed up the river.

Even it had a place to dock.

Disorientated, it took me a moment to remember where I was. I lay beneath my covers staring out at the sky-light above me. The darkness of the night was making way for a warm pink morning horizon. I wished I could stay there forever, not confronting any of the hard decisions I knew were waiting for me.

I wanted to stay and look through my newfound portal. I wanted to watch as birds flew by and stars filled the frame again. Surprisingly, I was looking forward to going to school! Perhaps it would make me feel normal? I grabbed some clothes and a towel from the set of drawers at the end of my bed. I still hadn't unpacked. I didn't want to appear comfortable or as if I was willing to accept that this is where I would be living for an extended amount of time. I snuck out of the bedroom, careful not to wake Claire. Mid-yawn, I entered the lounge room and was surprised to see Ian. The light in the kitchen was on and he was sitting at the table reading.

"Good morning Stacey! Bright and early!"

His positivity was almost sickening at this time of the day. His face lit up every time he smiled and there was so much light in his eyes. I had never quite seen that before... a reflection of pure joy from someone's eyes.

"Morning..."

As soon as the bathroom door closed behind me, I slid to the floor. I didn't want Ian to notice any sign of weakness, and I sure as hell didn't want Claire to see me vulnerable! With her still in bed, I knew this was a safe place for a while. I rested my head on the side of the shower wall and watched the water run down the drain. I wanted to scream and punch the glass but I knew that was completely stupid.

Goddamn it, Stacey! Pull yourself together!

I walked back out to the kitchen... and Ian was still sitting there.

Still reading.

Still smiling.

I needed to psych myself up for the day, and my regular early morning vodka shots were definitely not an option here. Coffee was the next best thing, so I made a long black and took a seat next to Ian.

"What time do you start school today?"

He highlighted something in his book, which incidentally was the Bible. It made me cringe... firstly because I hate doodling in books and secondly, because God and the whole religion thing was just plain weird.

Why was Ian reading this book for such a long time? He was sitting there before my shower... and here he is... still reading! Are you supposed to read the Bible in one sitting? Fuck that!

"First class is at 8.30am. I'll leave soon so I get there on time."

He laughed and closed the Bible.

"Don't be silly! I'll take you today! I'm sure Claire won't mind if I duck out for five minutes. I'll chuck some washing on the line and we'll leave in twenty, okay?"

Shit! 'Thou shall not walk to school?' Is that a commandment?

I did not want to take him up on his offer, but decided to let my ego lose this one. So I agreed. It was still early when Ian was done, so we sat on the couch making general conversation. He soon began to share his faith and how he thought the "big man" upstairs had all of us residents protected. Different religions fascinate me, so my curiosity was open to hearing what he believed. I had studied a Religion class the previous year at school, but my knowledge of Christianity was miniscule. I was more interested in Islam and Buddhism. Sure, I listened to Lecrae every now and then... but I didn't understand what the lyrics were implying. I mean, hell!!! I would be one of the last people to walk in to a church!!! As I was reaching to pick up my backpack, Ian asked if he could pray for me. Even though I hated God, Christians, and all their associated bullshit, I still thought it was a nice gesture for someone to offer to pray for me. I had heard I lived a life that was sending me straight to hell, so it was kind that this person (who probably shunned me as a dirty sinner) would want to put in a good word for me.

"Ah, yeah... sure."

I had been to Sunday school a few times with my childhood best friend; but it was more like a day care service, so I didn't learn anything. We had a few religion classes at primary school, too. Again, I learned nothing. I assumed Christians prayed when they went to bed. Didn't they get down on their knees, utter the words "Dear God," say a few sentences, seal it with a sweet "Amen" and then nod off to sleep? So when Ian placed his hand on my shoulder and began praying out loud... I was creeped out!

I couldn't quite understand why his prayer was so lengthy and casual in manner. Surely somewhere in his Bible, it has specific prayers to say. I was quite certain this conversational prayer wouldn't be found in there! He prayed a blessing over me, for my day at school and the days to come and that I would have peace-of-mind when decisions came up during the week. He finished with an "Amen" (I was right about something) and then walked out the door!

Weird.

I was so thankful to see my school as we pulled up. I couldn't exit the car fast enough! For the next five hours I wanted to pretend the last two days had never happened. All I wanted to do was cry but I didn't want my friends to be more concerned about me. They had never seen me cry before until Saturday night when, in all my drunken glory, I was absolutely distressed at how messed-up things were.

Put on the mask, Stacey. Let them know you're fine. You can do this.

I played it cool and acted like a heartless bitch when people asked me questions. I made it seem like I didn't care my entire world had been shaken and ripped out from under me. I tried all I could to get through the day without falling into a heap. I also couldn't stop thinking about Ian praying for me before school. I joked about it with my friends and even mimicked him with my best mates. They all thought I was locked up in some crazy Christian-run youth shelter. I wasn't going to disagree.

CHAPTER THREE

I wanted to burst in to tears as soon as I saw Mel's face. Instead, I gritted my teeth and attempted to slow my breathing. "Oh darling! Come on through."

I didn't know what I was going to tell her. She knew I was going to be at the shelter in a couple of weeks and we had been talking about the whole process for months, but she wasn't expecting me to pull the trigger so soon.

Why DID I pull the trigger so soon?! I'm so fucking stupid!!!

The walk to Mel's office felt like the longest I have taken in my entire life. So many thoughts were whirling through my mind, I was trying to pluck one out so I could talk to her. But I couldn't. My mind was a blur.

"How are you going?"

Fucking terrible!

"Yeah, alright I guess. I just don't really know what to do."

If only Mel could wave her magic wand (that all therapists have, obviously!) and make everything better. I didn't want to be scared anymore. I didn't want to cry anymore. I didn't want to be in this turmoil anymore.

Please, Mel.

"The shelter is okay, I guess. There's only me and one other resident there at the moment. She seems pretty chill so that's cool. I hate the portion size of tea, though. It makes me feel like crap. I hated it."

That's it? Seriously?! Everything I'm going through and all I manage to say is how the portion size of a meal is making me feel crap?

I had serious issues with food but was convinced I didn't have an eating disorder. Mel could tell I was freaking out about the meals and said she would email Ian to fill him in on some of the stuff I was going through so I could relax a bit better.

Awesome.
Wave that magic wand anytime, Mel. Any damn time you please!

I couldn't bring myself to tell her just how torn apart I was about my parents. I didn't want to regurgitate that Saturday morning and the last words my mother said to me. I certainly didn't want to explain how she took my house key off me, making it harder to return for the belongings I had left behind. I felt like complete shit and hated both my parents, yet I still had so much love for them. I was conflicted... big time. Ultimately I hated myself the most, though and I blamed myself for every single thing that led to me leaving home. I had no idea what was going to happen. I didn't know if I was ever going to see them again. I had nowhere to call home. I was an alcoholic, depressed, abused, broken, confused, homeless seventeen-year-old teenage girl. If the odds weren't stacked against me before, they definitely were now! Had I voluntarily made life one hundred times worse by leaving my parents' house?

"It's going to be okay. You're such a strong, brave girl. Just take it one day at a time... You're going to get through this."

I leaned back in the chair and stared at Mel. I knew she could see straight through the mask I was wearing. After almost a year of sessions, she had learnt all my lies... and she knew that coaxing me to remove the mask was going to be a challenge.

"How did everything go at work on Saturday?"

Shit! Work!

I didn't know what days I was rostered on for that week. I didn't even know if I had the strength to go back to my hometown. The shelter was about a twenty-minute drive from where I grew up, which gave me at least a few kilometers of breathing space. I loved my job, and I loved my boss and colleagues even more. Working in retail definitely isn't a breeze, especially in a small town full of unusual folk. However, work had become my safe haven — as much as I struggled with it at times, I was able to forget about everything for a few hours. I had so much fun with my colleagues. Everyone had just the right balance of work and play. I owed so much to my boss. Saturday morning when I had left my parent's house, I had rocked up to work ready to open the shop, laden with a bag of clothes, all my school books, blood shot eyes from crying... and a smile ready to serve the customers. I insisted I was fine, however my boss knew things were going to get out of hand really quickly if I stayed.

"Horrible." I responded.

"I didn't work. I ended up meeting the boys."

I had the most amazing group of guy friends. They meant the world to me. Sure, they probably weren't the most popular or good-looking guys around, but they were my mates and I loved them. We had arranged to go camping after I finished work, but I rang them when my boss told me she wasn't going to let me work my shift. They knew things at home were tough, but they never pried to find out details. They also knew vodka was my go-to (we had nick named it my "red baby," due to the Smirnoff label...) and so when they picked me up, we went to the bottle shop immediately. I didn't want them to see me cry. I didn't want them to know how petrified I was.

Just down your red baby, Stacey. You can do this. Don't cry... just drink.

Mel's face softened sympathetically as I poured my heart out. I still couldn't express how scared I really was, but I knew she could tell... despite my best efforts to hide.

"It's going to be okay, darling. It's all going to be okay."

CHAPTER FOUR

The campus Police officer wrote down every word tumbling from my trembling lips. I didn't want to get the authorities involved and even though I was three months away from turning eighteen, I was worried I was breaking the law. I didn't want to alert child protection or be forced back home. Thankfully, I was "of legal age to leave home" and unless I wanted to press charges, no further action would be taken. I clenched my teeth until they almost shattered. The officer was asking me to explain in more detail what my home life was like. His office space was shared with several other teachers and I was glad a support teacher was at her desk. It was comforting knowing there was a female nearby. When I had finally opened up my story to Mel, I hadn't been able to put the events into words... I felt as if my voice box had taken off in panic. I had to write everything down.

What if I can't tell him what happened? What if my voice escapes me again?

I blamed myself for everything: for every hand that was placed on me, for every word spewed over me, for every tear my mother cried, and all the pain my parents were probably feeling right now. Every child thinks the world of their parents, regardless of the horrible things they may have done. Despite everything, I still desired the best for them. I had to convince myself to believe what I was doing was the right thing to do.

"If you want to press charges, know you have the support of us all. The boys in blue will be in your corner."

I knew that pressing charges would result in a court trial, and I knew that would destroy my parents. I also didn't want to sabotage my brother's life. I just wanted to file a report, inform the local authorities I wasn't missing (like they had been led to believe), and somehow move forward with life. The officer told me he would visit my parents later that day to have a chat and let them know I was safe. From what he was telling me, I had no reason to fear they would try to contact me or find where I was staying.

Bullshit! We live on the coast of a small island state… I am taking refuge only twenty minutes from their house… My workplace is only three minutes away… Plenty of people know I am at the shelter, and gossip is vicious in this small town!

I didn't take his word for it.

I knew I had to watch my own back. I knew from now on, the only person I could rely on was myself. It was my word against theirs, and I knew manipulation was a generational trait in my family. If I wanted to stay on the front foot, I had to prepare for things to get very nasty.

"Wanna play a game?"

A guy who was too old to be a resident stood in front of the pool table. I had no idea why he was there.

"Ugh, sure."

I snatched the pool cue and leaned against the table as he collected the balls from each corner pocket. Playing pool was the only thing to do in this place. I would have preferred if he offered me a gram of weed, though... that would have been more entertaining.

"I'm Justin, nice to meet you."

He offered his hand, so I reached across the table and shook it. I always made it a point to greet someone with a strong handshake, that way they get the message up front that I'm not a pushover!

"Hey man. I'm Stacey."

I soon realized that Justin had a decent pool game and wondered if he perfected his skills while staying at the shelter, too.

"I was here not too long ago but by God's Grace I was saved!"

Oh fucking hell! Another crazy Christian! What the hell is this place?! Did Ian set this whole thing up?!

I aimed my shot up and smiled at him before knocking two balls straight in to the corner end pocket.

"Do you listen to Lecrae?"

Fuck.

"Yeah man, I do sometimes."

I handed him the cue and folded my arms as I watched him take his turn. What was he trying to do? Brainwash me as we played pool? Was I supposed to be some crazy Christian by the end of this game?

"You should come to church with me one week."

I'm not doing a damn thing with you, mate.

"Ugh, yeah. Maybe."

I quickly finished the game, hoping he would leave me alone. To my disappointment he ended up wanting a rematch — he wasn't going to let a girl beat him! I lost interest not long after we started the second game and attempted to wrangle more information out of him. Before I knew it, Justin was telling me his story and "by God's Grace I'm saved." Remarkably, the more he talked, the more intrigued I became.

Maybe he wasn't such a weird, crazy Christian. But I was still skeptical. Why would he want to come and hang out at the shelter, though? I would rather wear a frilly pink dress and go to a day spa than spend my free time in this hell hole! I admired his vulnerability to open up to a stranger, and I appreciated he was willing to make me feel like I wasn't alone.

Maybe he was right, maybe I wasn't alone.

Even though we shared some similarities, he still didn't know what it felt like to live this life. Hell, he didn't know a single thing about my life or how I ended up at the shelter - and I refused to tell him!

"I'm just saying... God can do this for you, as well. He is so good and I praise him every day and pray you can encounter His Goodness, Stacey."

What was I going to do? I couldn't tell him to go get fucked. He had just poured his heart out and unpacked his entire life story. Sure, I was interested about Christianity and to hear more about God... but I just thought it was bizarre... this random guy coming to hang out at the shelter, play pool, and talk about Jesus. Surely he had another agenda. People aren't nice like that without reason.

CHAPTER FIVE

Time in the shelter had a funny way of slowing down until I could almost hear the second hand scraping! Week two rolled around and I was faced with the certainty of staying until a house of my own became available. There was a 'no drug and alcohol' policy at the shelter; but I had little respect for that. Compared to some of the other residents, I found it easier to fly under the radar. I knew just what to say and how to act so the workers were oblivious to what I was really up to. Claire had left to go to another shelter, but a new girl, Rachel, had arrived... and we became friends almost instantly. The workers emphasized the importance of still attending school, however, it was the last thing I wanted to be doing. Here's the clincher though: our school attendance, behavior toward the workers, and general attitude at the shelter all contributed to how fast one would get their own place to live. I wasn't a fan of the workers, except for Ian and Georgina (who happened to be a Christian too); but I was determined to do all it took to guarantee I would get my own home as soon as possible. I knew it would most likely take a couple of months before I could leave.

I decided to return to work, even though I was still feeling emotionally weak and raw. I had missed my co-workers so much, I almost burst into tears as I walked through the doors on my first day back. It felt so good to be surrounded by this familiar routine and environment. I knew how to provide exceptional customer service and was stoked to forget about all other drama for the next four hours. The Police had spoken to my parents over the previous three weeks, and so I was not expecting any trouble as I worked my afternoon shifts. Work was like my safe bubble that blocked anything bad from getting in. Thirty minutes until closing time, I was serving on the register. There were two other workers... one was tidying the store and the other was out back. Those final thirty minutes are either incredibly busy or painfully slow. That night, it was painfully slow. I kept checking my watch, counting down the minutes until I could make the closing call. I left the register and decided to spend the last couple of minutes straightening the batteries... what better way to waste time! Ten minutes before closing, I heard the doors open. Smiling wide to welcome a customer and gently remind them we were closing soon, I looked up. My brain took a moment to register the face walking towards me, and my heart started pounding.

It was my father.

Thankfully I was adjacent to a pillar so I quickly ducked behind it, hoping he hadn't seen me. I didn't have time to process him just showing up... My mind was spinning out suggestions: I wanted to scream. I wanted to camouflage into the pillar. I wanted to run.

RUN!

I dropped the batteries and legged toward the staff room. I told my co-worker to jump on the register. My hands were shaking and sweaty, and it took me two times to correctly enter the pin code to the staffroom. I made a beeline to the security cameras and watched as my dad looked down every aisle, searching for me.

I felt nauseous. This was my safe place. The bad stuff couldn't come through those doors.

This was my safe place. This was my safe place. This was my god damn safe place!!

I held my breath as he walked past the staff room, and began to cry as he passed through the register and out the door. He didn't say a single word to the co-worker who had taken my place. I hated being so fearful. I wished I could stand tall and strong and simply tell my parents I wasn't coming home. In that moment, part of me wanted to take them to Court. Maybe pressing charges was actually the right thing to do, after all? At least then my safe place would stay my safe place.

A punching bag hung in the middle of the laundry room - my victim for the night. I knew I had to do something before the worker on shift tonight tried to make me talk about what was going on. I felt so incredibly weak and mentally exhausted, but my blood was pumping and I needed to punch something. I jumped up and down and started swinging my arm.

"FUCK YOU!"

Every hit became harder. Every word that fell from my mouth filled with more anger.

"Fuck you! Fuck you! FUCK YOU!!!"

Footsteps approached the laundry room as I waltzed around the punching bag. My eyes were so fixated on the face my imagination had plastered across the bag, I didn't look up to see who entered.

"Do you want some boxing gloves?"

The worker stood at the door, gloves in hand ready to strap them on.

No I don't want boxing gloves! I don't care if I hurt myself! I hope I break my fucking wrist!!!

"No, I'm fine."

He stood there for a while as I continued slamming into the bag. He was probably relieved I was venting my rage in a healthy manner, instead of drinking or self-harming. He probably saw this all the time: damaged, depressed, unwanted kids, out in the laundry room at night, trying to figure out where to go when their life was swirling down the gutter. I was willing every ounce of my inside-pain to leave through each blow to the punching bag. There was so much anger mounting within, and it only felt as though it was building. It seemed impossible to alleviate... even the slightest. I kept punching until I fell to the floor, sobbing and clutching my hand, now swollen and bloodied. For three weeks I had been convincing myself I was strong enough to get through. Every morning I woke telling myself I was brave and capable of facing the day. I was kidding myself! I was in a battle I knew I couldn't run from.

As I walked out from the laundry room, I determined to don a brave face. I was going to try to not care about anything anymore.

Could I write a letter to the universe stating my surrender? White flag drawn... *I am done!*

Except for the worker and one other resident, the house was empty. Trying to hold myself together, I sat on the couch opposite him. Earlier that day, we had told each other why we were in the shelter. He hadn't said anything when I told him why I was there; but as I held my bloody knuckle, I saw the way he was looking at me, and I knew he was going to bring it back up.

"Why did you let them touch you though? I would've killed the bastards if they ever tried to do that to me!"

How could I let them touch me? Why didn't I leave sooner?

I found solace in the fact the residents there were probably the least judgmental people you will ever come across. How can you judge someone else's life when your own is just as turbulent? Although some of the younger ones probably wouldn't appreciate the life discussions, the majority of people were down to talk about things. I liked knowing that although we'd all been through different situations, we knew what it was like to be screwed over by the people who should have been there for us.

"I don't know man, it's just complicated."

I pushed up from the couch and walked to the kitchen to get a drink. I didn't know what else to tell him. What if he thought

I was weak? What if he thought I would just lay down and take shit from anyone?

"I mean, you shouldn't let them get away with it, Stace! That's messed up!"

I wanted to cry. I wanted to cry so fucking badly. I haven't even gone into details and he already knows it's messed up! How did I think it was acceptable?! Why did I let it go on for such a long time?!

"Want a drink man?"

"Na, but I do want to fucking punch them! What bastards!"

I laughed, hoping he was serious and would go serve 'justice' in the way I so fervently wanted it to be served.

"You can't take that crap! You have to stand up for yourself!"

Isn't it strange what we let some people do to us? I wouldn't allow anyone else to treat me so poorly. I wouldn't allow another hand be placed upon me like that. How contradictory that I would remain quiet and let things escalate to such extremes. I wouldn't hesitate to fight someone who started violating me... in any state. I wouldn't pussyfoot at all.

Why the fuck did I let them do it?! Why did I think love meant being quiet and letting people do whatever they wanted? Why didn't I say anything? Why didn't I leave sooner? Why didn't I yell louder? Why didn't they see the bruises? Why didn't anyone notice anything? Why did I blame it all on myself?! I.am.a.fucking.idiot!!!

"I know."

He shook his head in disbelief, as if he didn't think I was capable of standing up for myself... as if I wasn't capable of protecting myself.

"Well, at least you're out now. Fuck 'em all! That's what I say. Fucking bastards! Make 'em regret ever laying a hand on you!"

CHAPTER SIX

I had gone from a straight A, award winning, top-of-the-class student in high school, to a college kid who failed to submit assignments and hardly turned up to class. Plummeting into depression, attending class was becoming a serious struggle. Losing myself in marijuana and drinking my red baby again, my thoughts were tormenting; and the last thing I was concerned about was fulfilling assignment due dates. My teachers were now aware my life was in tatters and tried to accommodate me any way they could. My favorite, an English Writing teacher, was an amazing help! In an effort to ease my anxieties and allow me space and quiet to get work done, he agreed to mark me as present while I did my work in a nearby classroom. I sat in the vacant room, my English assignments piled around me, commiserating on where it all went wrong. In dead silence, I doodled over an empty page. Even though I was physically present, my mind was elsewhere. I was drowning in homework, assignments, and coursework needed for end of year assessment. I suspected I wasn't going to get my Year 12 certificate.

How could I make it through another term, let alone to the end of the year?

I was probably going to drop out as soon as I left the shelter. The only reason I was still trying was so the workers thought I was doing well... and I could get my own place. I ripped up the paper and stared at a fresh piece. I started to write... From the very top of the page to bottom, every inch was soon covered.

I want to die. I want to die.

~

That night, a worker who I didn't particularly like, was rostered on. Still fearful of the food servings, I didn't want this worker to make me feel like crap about dinner, so I told her I wouldn't be back until curfew. I wandered through the streets until it got dark and decided to go to Hungry Jacks. I struggled eating around people, so going to Hungry Jacks was risky, but that night there wasn't anyone eating in. I sat against the back wall and chowed down a burger meal. It took almost forty minutes to consume a burger and small fries. After all the food I had eaten over the past two weeks and then gorging on Hungry Jacks, I felt gross and miserable. I took my tray to the bin and headed to the toilets. There still wasn't anyone eating in the restaurant so I knew I had the all-clear. Locking the stall door behind me, I leaned over the bowl. I knew the exact angle my fingers had to be to make the gag most effective.

Two pumps and the entire meal was up.

I had never purged in a public restroom before. Hurling in a public toilet is disgusting, and I would have freaked if anyone walked in; but it was all I could do until I had my own place. The shelter wasn't safe enough... too many people could hear. As I stood, I felt oddly satisfied, knowing I had just gotten rid of all those calories. Since arriving at the shelter, I had been feeling pathetic about the amount of food I was agreeing to eat. The only solution was to go back to restricting food intake and conceal my purging. The difficulty I faced was the risk of the workers finding out. With a few kilograms to spare before the questions began, I could keep my behavior under the radar until

I reached my next goal weight. As I stood at the basin washing my hands, I was disappointed with myself for not engaging in my usual patterns. It was time to bring them all back again.

I walked the two blocks to Kmart to gather supplies. On the nights I wasn't able to bring up what I ate, I would punish myself. And those times I didn't restrict as much as I resolved to, I would hurt myself to counteract all the 'mistakes.' Punishment would come in the form of an open wound... the only way I know how to punish myself when I fall back on all other punishments. Up until this point, I had veiled my self-harm scars under clothing. But now I no longer cared. I knew my wrist was a fresh canvas and a lot easier to access during stressful times. I was on a train of self-destruction... heading toward a destination of no return. When I wasn't thinking rationally, hurting myself was the only way I knew how to cope. I had lost everything and this was the only thing remaining that I felt I could control. Cutting was just another way I thought I could cope. It relieved feelings of stress and discomfort, and while inside I was incredibly numb, at least the stinging sensation allowed me to feel something. It was also a lot easier to hide cuts than undercover vomiting or skipping meals.

I still had an hour until curfew, so I sat at the beach, convincing myself the words I had written earlier that day were my destiny. But logistically, my plan was going to be challenging whilst still living at the shelter. I didn't have the courage to actually kill myself. I wish I did. My heart was too big, and I was always scared I would hurt people if I were to kill myself. I had plans of how I would end my life if I ever woke up one day with enough strength to do it. However I was always so careful to plan out who would find me. I didn't want to totally destroy a stranger's life, which ruled out jumping off a bridge or hanging myself in a tree. I also didn't like the idea of a friend or loved one finding me if I happened to do it once I got my own house. I didn't want to make a bloody mess, either. I constantly thought about how I would do it and wanted to make sure I had thought through every possible scenario.

My focus shifted to a group of people enjoy their evening out in a nearby restaurant. I wondered what their lives were like. I sifted sand through my fingertips as I imagined what it would be like to live in their shoes. I would have done anything to switch places with anyone in that restaurant.

I got back to the shelter just before curfew. Relieved with my new supplies, I slipped in to bed. Staring up through the skylight, like every other night, I made sure Rachel was fast asleep before I let myself cry. As much as I wanted to keep destroying myself, I fiercely wished for everything to be okay. I wanted there to be another way to cope with things. I wanted to know there was a way out of this... a way that would make life good.

Who was I kidding?

Using the moonlight to guide my reach, I found my Kmart supplies — tucked secretly into a book on my bedside table. I took the new silver blade and held its glinting, cold edge between my thumb and forefinger...

CHAPTER SEVEN

Somewhere along the line, I agreed to begin alcohol counselling. Apparently seeing Mel almost weekly wasn't enough support (although technically I was going to Mel for everything other than alcohol...) maybe the workers were right to suggest I see someone, but I sure as hell wasn't going to admit I had an issue! I thought if I remained compliant, the chances of me getting out of the shelter and into my own house would increase. I had no intention to stop drinking. I was getting drunk almost every night, which is probably why the workers suggested counselling. Apparently I woke Rachel one night because I was being obnoxiously loud. I was too wasted to consider holding the bottle instead of plonking it back on my bedside table every ten minutes.

The first session with my alcohol worker was horrible. I was so tired of opening up and talking about my crap life. Besides, I only wanted to disclose all of the pain to Mel. I wasn't interested with having all these other unknowns up in my personal business! The worker taught me strategies I could use to avoid drinking as much. She also asked if I was using any other drugs to cope. I laughed and brushed off her question.

"Oh, only occasionally at parties."

She didn't need to know I was getting high almost every day. The less she knew, the better.

I wanted this as painless as possible. I wasn't doing these sessions because I actually desired to control my alcohol consumption; it was only for the workers benefit so they thought I was genuinely interested in bettering myself.

I had about three sessions before I reached a new low.

One night I decided to start drinking before everyone went to bed. There were two other residents at the shelter: boys. We were outside having a smoke and they knew I was pretty wasted. They convinced me to sneak the vodka outside so they could have some too. Sharing is caring, so I agreed. We all knew this was going to be an easy task to pull off because the worker on shift that night was the most oblivious of the team. I walked inside, trying to act normal. The workers were fine with residents smoking just as long as we went under the gazebo area, so going back outside wasn't going to raise suspicion. I shoved the bottle down my top and pulled on a hoodie to try to obscure the obvious. The worker was still watching television as I passed.

Success!

Considering I was the eldest, I should have been setting a better example; but when you're living in a shelter, favors are currency. You help someone out, they help you. Forming friendships was as valuable as gold and you certainly didn't want to get on anyone's wrong side. By now, I was so immune to the alcohol that I couldn't tell the difference between water and vodka. However, I soon discovered that is not normal. The boys couldn't handle the burn of straight shots, so we were done sooner than I thought. What pussies!

"Stacey..."

Shit!

As soon as I was putting the cap on the bottle, the worker was making her way to the door. The boys distracted her for a second while I attempted to jam the bottle back up my top. I couldn't afford to be sprung! If I was going to avoid getting caught, I had to pull some magic bullshit out of my ass. I walked around the corner... with each step the bottle was inching out of my top. Hunched against the door, I tried maneuvering the bottle without alerting the worker.

"You're down to cook tea tomorrow. Do you want to see what's in the pantry?"

She knows something is up!

I leaned into the wall as I shuffled past her. It probably looked suss as hell, but it was the only way I could keep the vodka from falling out and not blow our cover.

"Umm yeah, okay. I just got to go pee. I'm busting!!"

Still clutching the wall, I skulked past her and then bolted to the bathroom. As I turned into the hallway, I caught the bottle just before it hit the floor. I was freaking out... where would I hide it?! I couldn't go to my room in case she followed. I couldn't leave it out for everyone to see. The bathroom drawers! Problem solved! Thankfully, it did fit! After I pulled off the what-I-want-to-cook-for-dinner act, I went for a shower — the perfect ploy for bottle retrieval! Wrapped snuggly in a towel and carried back to my room, my ruse went undetected.

~

The next night, I risked getting caught again. The previous evening's shenanigans were way too close for my liking. Besides, I wasn't keen on implicating the other residents. Rachel was fast asleep, as usual, and I had learnt the other night she didn't appreciate being disturbed while I drank. It was about 11pm and I was convinced the worker was in bed. I had already drained about a third of the vodka as I stood with my ear to the door, listening for any stirrings. After convincing myself the coast was clear, I snuck from my room toward the bathroom. As I crept closer to the lounge room, I realized my error. My hearing had let me down... big time. All the lights were on and the worker was still up, sitting on the lounge room floor watching T.V.

Play it cool, Stace, don't blow it.

I am basically a pro at drunk walking; but this time I was caught off guard. At the very moment the worker glanced up, my legs failed me! He asked if I was okay, so I casually idled before attempting another few steps.

"Just... going to the loo."

Not only did I almost trip over the couch, but I almost tripped over the worker too. If he couldn't tell I had been drinking, he was just as ignorant as the worker from last night. With the bathroom door closed, I sprawled across the floor, smiling from ear to ear. I had my phone with me, but I couldn't even tell the time. The numbers blurred together and for all I knew I could have been in there for half an hour already.

Life is only bearable when I am drinking. When I'm sober, it's too painful and I don't know how to handle all the unpredictable anger.

For that moment in time, staring at the ceiling, I didn't have a care in the world. All my worries seemed to have faded away.

Vodka is always the answer. Always!

I don't remember making my way back to my bedroom. One second I was on the bathroom floor and the next, in bed, squinting at the morning.

CHAPTER EIGHT

After one month at the shelter, I was finally told I would be getting my own place! A unit had become available, so as soon as it was ready, I was out of here! I was stoked and decided to up my game by showing the workers I was challenging myself with alcohol recovery and making positive choices about my future. I was still seeing Mel fortnightly and making progress with her concerning a lot of my issues. Mel's therapy was top shelf quality. She had the perfect balance of everything you could ever want in a therapist: acceptance, compassion, wisdom, patience. I could talk so openly with Mel about everything that was going on, although the only thing I didn't disclose was how serious my suicidal thoughts were becoming. A worker at the shelter mentioned the cuts on my wrist being more frequent, and I'm sure Mel noticed them too.

I finally agreed with her reaching out to a sexual abuse counselling service. I sure as hell wasn't ready, but I thought if I went ahead with her recommendation, it would be another tick for my deceptive progress. I also decided to change alcohol workers. Not only because I didn't feel comfortable with my current one but I also thought the workers would think I actually cared about my recovery, and wanted to be sure I was getting the most out of each session. I was prepared to do whatever it took to move out of the shelter... even if that meant reopening some of the most painful wounds I had.

Knowing I could get away with drinking at the shelter, I attempted to risk purging. When I was the only resident, I successfully showed the worker I could eat a normal sized meal for tea. I played it cool, and snuck in to the bathroom while he watched T.V. I closed the door between the lounge room and hallway to help block any noise. I knew I could be making a terrible mistake, but I had to do something. I could feel every inch of fat on my bones and wanted to slice it all off. Kneeling in front of the toilet, I made sure I couldn't hear any footsteps before I threw up the chicken and vegetables. Euphoria washed over me as I stared into the toilet bowl. The motion of heaving was disgusting, but had become such a big part of who I was. It was as normal to me as any other daily task. I no longer had to put much thought in to how to bring everything up. I was now a pro of my own self-destruction. I made sure I wasn't in the bathroom for too long and walked back out to the lounge, acting as if nothing had just occurred. I was nervous the worker would say he heard me, but no concerns were raised.

~

The first thing I bought for my house was a set of scales.

I was given a list of necessities to be deemed "secure" enough to move in: cutlery, bed and linen topped the list... but all I cared about was scales. The thought of having my own place to live excited me so much. Knowing I would be able to purge whenever I wanted, skip meals without being questioned, cut and not have to hide it all the time, and get drunk without sneaking around! The freedom sounded exhilarating! I stood in the bathroom aisle of Kmart for almost twenty minutes, trying to work out which scale would be the best. I had limited funds, but justified paying an extra $10 for a digital set of scales compared to an ordinary analogue one. I wanted to be able to record my weight correctly, gram by gram. Even the slightest change in my weight mattered. I would also have free reign to finally start reaching my goal weight quicker. I didn't have to worry so much about other people, and wearing baggy clothes would keep me from raising any suspicion. The only other thing I bought before leaving Kmart was cutlery... to show the workers I was thinking about eating and committed to being healthy.

It wasn't until my last fortnight in the shelter that I finally bought everything on the list. I ended up going to the Salvation Army, who gave me a couch, bed and linen free of charge! I hated handouts and I would have been quite content with sleeping on the floor until I could afford a bed. But to make the 'authorities' happy and guarantee I could leave the shelter, I agreed to the handouts and got everything they suggested.

I still only liked two of the workers: Georgina and Ian. One day Ian told me how he had MS (Multiple Sclerosis). I used to do the MS Read-a-thon every year in primary school and was well aware of what it was... and how there was no cure. So here was this crazy Christian, telling me he *had* MS.

Where the hell did it go?! Are you going to share this cure with the rest of the people suffering?! How is that even possible?!

He explained how he went for brain scans and it was clear... and when put next to previous scans, there was an obvious change; there was absolutely no signs left of MS!

"God healed me!"

Umm, what?! How can a God that lives in the clouds (or something like that...) heal an illness? If this was actually a true story, and God really did heal him, then why would God not make more people aware of the cure? How can someone who is make-believe do something real?

It made absolutely no sense to me and I started to think Ian *was* a crazy Christian after all. I was stupid to consider there was ever such a thing as a non-brainwashed preaching freak. Although I still had no answer as to why Georgina seemed so normal. Maybe she would tell me how she was healed of something next time I saw her. I listened to Ian, attempting to catch him out on any bullshit. But nothing came! The more he talked and told me more about how God heals, and how he wasn't the only person who had ever been healed by God, the more interested I became. Apparently, we're all God's children (because He created us all?) and He loves us all the same. I couldn't understand how He could love me equally as someone like Georgina. I had made so many mistakes and bad decisions on a daily basis... how could God look at me and want to love me, knowing I was such a failure compared to those who actually believed in Him?

People have walked out of my life, people who were supposed to love me all my life. Why would God stay by my side and never leave me?

I wasn't convinced about the whole God thing, but I certainly became more curious about Christianity. I knew Georgina went to a local church, so if some sort of miracle occurred (and apparently miracles are common with God!), I knew who to contact if I wanted to attend.

I paced back and forth in the small cubicle. These unhygienic walls had become a place where I could gather myself during panic attacks... where I felt safe to purge. I couldn't throw up in the shelter anymore because there were now too many residents, and I still had a couple more weeks before moving into my own place. I had put on a strong front around the dinner table to convince everyone I was doing fine; but after downing an entire meal, I hurriedly left the shelter. Public toilets were where my defenses came down and I could do what I was agitated to do throughout the day. These four walls protected me from the expectations of society, as well as what I demanded of myself. Within this space my mask peeled away and I could do everything I needed to make it through each day. I listened as the cubicle next to me became vacant, and footsteps disappeared.... then I punched the tiled wall and fell to my knees. I was breathing in deep gulps of air. It frustrated me that such an unhygienic place had become my 'safe haven'.

Disgusting bitch!!! Fat, ugly, worthless piece of shit!

Anyone could walk in — at any moment — but purging here was a lot safer than at the shelter. The toilet flushed just as I heard footsteps approaching. Leaning against the wall, I waited until I was alone again. I slowly opened the door and caught my reflection in the mirror. My hands were trembling and my eyes a bloodshot, watery mess. I had no idea who I was anymore. Sometimes I wished my heart wasn't as soft... I wished I didn't care about others so much. I wished I wasn't so concerned about everyone's feelings. I wished I was strong enough to end it all. Masquerading I was fine, was exhausting.

I wish I could be a bitch and vent what is going on inside, instead of bottling it all up and living this secret life.

I wished I could storm thorough the shelter doors and tell the workers I hated their guts. I wished I could punch every single person who said they loved me but insisted on beating me and tearing me apart. I wanted to scream at everyone who told me to calm down.

I hate the universe for throwing me shit cards. I hate that I'm so fucked up at such a young age.

I felt broken and destroyed in every way possible. There wasn't even the remotest reason why I wanted to be alive. I was caught in a self-destructive cycle — leading straight to the grave.

I am *soooo* ready to die.

CHAPTER NINE

I hauled the scales out of the box and headed to my bathroom. It felt so good to be in my own place: peace and quiet... uninterrupted! I told myself leaving the shelter would be a fresh start, that I would finally start taking recovery seriously. Deep down I wanted the best for my life, but the darkness was overpowering, and even my very best intentions couldn't rise to the surface and take over. Placing the scales on the floor, I grabbed a piece of paper and pen that would remain on the window sill: my official weight tally. I noted the date, stepped on the scales, and made my first official entry.

I hadn't yet found the energy to unpack the bags scattered across the lounge room floor. The only thing ready was my bed but I decided the couch would be sufficient to sleep on over the next few nights. My house didn't feel homely. I knew what a house was and how a house felt, but I didn't know what a home was or how a home was supposed to feel. I had a spare bedroom I hoped to turn into an art studio. I didn't think I was a great artist by any means, but I liked the idea of having an empty room to go crazy with whatever I wanted to express on paper. My house was in one of the worst areas in town; a breeding ground for generational poverty and addictions. I had no intention of finishing Year Twelve anymore. There was absolutely no point in even trying. Now I was in my own house, I could sense the end was near. I didn't need to bullshit as much because I wasn't under constant surveillance and although I didn't have the strength to kill myself just yet, I knew that day would fast approach.

I sat on the couch looking at everything I still had to unpack. It was amazing how, in just over two months, my collection of 'stuff' had grown from one bag of clothes and school books, to three big bags full of household items, clothing, and art supplies. There was a full-length mirror attached to the cupboard in the lounge room. I stood in front of it, analyzing my body. I hadn't looked at a full-length mirror since I left home. My face was more chiseled, apart from my cheeks, which appeared 'puffy' due to purging. My thighs had whittled down to straight pegs, and my bum was smaller. Even though my stomach swelled during the day from the excessive amount of water I drunk, I was thinner than ever.

You're disgusting! Hit that goal weight and then you'll be beautiful.

I felt deflated as I surveyed the room. A couch, table, chairs, and desk were the only pieces in the living/dining area of my house.

How am I supposed to create a home when I don't even know what a home feels like? More to the point, how the hell am I even supposed to afford the things one needs to create a 'homely environment.'

With bills piling up and limited funds, everything that I wanted to have to fill my home was all but a dream. I wanted a lounge suite and rugs on the floor. I wanted a hammock to hang outside to lay in. I wanted a desk to write at and decorations that could fill the empty spaces on the wall. I knew I could obtain some of these things... but I didn't want handouts. Handouts meant people were giving me sympathy and that was the last thing I wanted!

Out of all the things I conjured up in my mind to fill my home and to possibly make it "homely", the only things that I really wanted were all the belongings that I had been collecting for years in preparation to move out when I went to University (which was obviously, now, not going to happen)

I remembered the day I bought the most beautiful teapot I had ever laid eyes on. Normally I wouldn't spend so much money on something let alone a teapot and matching cups, but there was something about this particular teapot that I couldn't leave the store without buying. I was so excited to move out and make tea from it during my study breaks. I dreamt about the days I would be a journalist, sipping herbal tea from the matching cups. This teapot represented so much. My independence, my future! It was also one of the first things I bought after starting my job in retail. In fact, I had collected countless kitchen gadgets that made me anticipate becoming a housewife one day. I would spend my time off, looking at what to add to my accumulating household items. And now I didn't have a single thing. It was all back at my parent's home. I closed my eyes and started to cry.

I was crying over a goddamn tea pot!

I remembered the pattern, and how the vibrant colors swirled and intertwined with each other, wrapping intricately around the smooth porcelain curves. The cups weren't like the normal ones I would usually drink my tea from. They were smaller, without a handle, and made me feel sophisticated as I cradled them in my hands. I squeezed my eyes tighter and began imagining everything that was in my room... everything I no longer had... everything I would never see again. I wanted to be wrapped in my chocolate brown blanket that would comfort me on a bleak winter's night. It was softer than anything I had ever felt and the perfect size to snuggle into. I wanted the posters that covered my bedroom walls. I wanted all the books lining my bookshelf, the novels and picture books that served as a form of escape throughout my childhood. I wanted the box of letters and presents my pen pal Hannah had sent me over the last four years.

As I remembered what I had left behind, I began sobbing. I had no idea if I would ever get them back. I had no idea if I would ever go back!

My record player and records, framed Beatles poster, signed Year Six school shirt, and High School Leavers Dinner dress (even though I would never dare to wear it again...) I just wanted it all back! Baby photos. My favorite coffee mug. All the clothes I couldn't fit into my bag.

I don't fucking care if wanting everything is selfish or stupid. I just want to feel normal. I just want something familiar. This life is now so foreign and scary and I just want to start again. I want to do it over — leave again — this time making sure I think first about what to bring! I want to have that day over.

How the hell is a teenager supposed to build a life from one bag of clothes and school books?!

My house was a two-minute walk to a small grocery store and soon I was visiting there almost daily. I had locked into a cycle of binging and purging. I wouldn't eat during the day, and then at night I would scoff more down in one sitting than was healthy... or normal. It was as if I was in a trance during the binging. I absolutely hated myself every single second, but while I was packing food into my face, I dissociated from the present. It was a race to see how much food I could consume until I snapped out of the trance-like state and realized what I had just done. I would always spend at least thirty minutes post-binge, sprawled out on the bathroom floor. I made sure I got rid of my entire stomach contents, forcing myself to puke until all that came up was water and flecks of blood. Mel didn't know how bad I was getting, mainly because I didn't want to admit I had an eating disorder. I was slowly closing in on my goal weight and knew when I reached it, Mel would notice and most likely discuss my situation. Until then, I was determined to keep doing all I could to put myself through hell.

Depression soon pulled me in tighter than ever before and I convinced my school to let me finish Year Twelve online. I had no intention of actually finishing the year. My plan was to gradually disconnect so when the time came to end it all, I wouldn't raise suspicion. I was still seeing my alcohol worker, Lindsay, as well as Mel almost weekly, which meant if I could see them on consecutive days, I would easily have almost five days without drawing attention... or before people became concerned. Overdosing seemed like the best option, so I started to plan the details.

My eighteenth year would be my last.

I had lost contact with most of my good friends, mainly because I knew they would catch on that I wasn't coping and be on my back. In times past, I had blamed the shelter when I went

MIA, but now I had my own place there were no excuses for not inviting people over – so I excused myself because of an excessive load of schoolwork which I always happened to be behind in. The only people who really kept tabs on me were Snezna and Jill. Even though Snezna lived in Sydney, and Jill in California, they would text and email to ask how I was going. Jill would occasionally call... just to check I was doing as well as I pretended in my emails. Snezna was the boss of the company I interned at for almost six years, and Jill was in charge of the majority of operations in America. They were the only role models I had in my life. The only women who I could look up to and genuinely know they loved me and wanted the very best for me. I knew it would break their hearts if they were aware of what was really going on. A part of me was thankful they lived so far away, but another part of me wished they could be right next door. I hated knowing they would have to find out about my death from a stranger and I knew they would be pissed I had lied to them. The thought of ever disappointing the two women who never once gave up on me was upsetting.

I lived one block from a highway and calculated my secondary plan was to jump off the bridge. I still didn't want to ruin anyone else's life by dragging them in to a gruesome event, but I knew the highway wasn't busy during the early hours, so I could jump without causing too much of a scene. Every time I walked over a bridge, I wondered how much it would hurt to jump. I inched closer to the railing and gazed at the road below me... picturing how my body would break... and wondering if my brains would splatter all over the place. Or would that only happen if I jumped in front of a car? I visualized how it would feel in the moments I was free falling. I had heard overdosing wasn't pain free; but that was my first preference. If I ended up in hospital for an attempted suicide because the OD failed... then the bridge jump would be my second chance.

Despite my best efforts to hide my spiralling emotions and behavior, Mel could see straight through me. I was lying through my teeth and it made me feel sick.

"Maybe going to the hospital for a short stay might help. You won't have to be there for a long time... just to have a break and a good rest."

No way! Everyone knows that's where all the crazies end up!

In primary school I was told if you take someone to the psych ward, you get fifty bucks! Maybe Mel receives a bonus for every client she admits...

"Na, I'm okay. Really!"

I wanted to cry. Had Mel finally realized I was beyond repair? Was she giving up on me? Was I really so messed up that the only place for me was the psych ward... surrounded by whack jobs?!

"If it's like the movie '*Girl, Interrupted*' I'll go!"

I chuckled, hoping my sarcasm would distract Mel from the sadness seeping through me. I wasn't going to hospital unless I was DOA (that is, Dead. On. Arrival!!).

There is no way I'm checking myself in while I'm still breathing. Hell no!

"Just think about it, okay?"

"Yeah."

I spent the rest of the session convincing Mel I was fine. I pretended I was using the positive coping mechanisms I had been taught and that they were helping to some extent. I knew Mel just wanted me to be healthy and happy, but the dilemma was... I didn't. I couldn't be healthy without feeling fat, and I certainly couldn't be happy without drinking.

"You're not weak for admitting you need help. It's actually quite brave to admit you need support. I just don't want you to do anything stupid before I see you next. Promise you won't? Promise you will come back next week... in one piece? Promise?"

"I promise."

CHAPTER TEN

My seventeenth year on this earth was hell. The week of my eighteenth birthday was soon approaching and I felt upset it wasn't going to be the major celebration I had always imagined. I spent the last day of seventeen making vodka gummy treats and stocking my fridge with drinks and munchies. Mel had planned a meeting with Lindsay on my birthday morning which was the only thing I had planned for the day. If I didn't have to wake up early to attend the meeting, I would have stayed in bed — all day — eating my vodka gummies and drinking. I didn't sleep at all... which was something that had become a common occurrence. I was having the occasional nightmare and some nights I didn't want to sleep because I knew depression would pin me to the bed in the morning. Around 5am, I started drinking and by the time Lindsay came and picked me up to take me to Mel's office, I was already pretty wasted. It was 8:40am. She was twenty minutes early and I was still trying to get ready. I couldn't focus for longer than a few minutes without getting distracted. Stumbling to the door, I welcomed Lindsay with a louder than appropriate "Hello."

"Oh dear... when did you start drinking?"

The irony of being drunk in the presence of your alcohol worker! My first day being eighteen was off to a great start! I clutched the railing as I walked down the front steps. I wasn't drunk enough to make a complete idiot of myself... I still had self-control and could (somewhat) understand what was happening around me. Mel was discussing their plan on how to best help me. The meeting was basically for the two of them — going over what they had talked about with me and what techniques I was being taught. I guess they wanted me to hear everything and to get my approval and thoughts. I didn't contribute much to the conversation, I was zoning out and trying to distract myself from a pressing need to pee.

"Are you okay?"

I didn't even realize Lindsay had left the room! Mel was looking at me, concerned — trying to read me like she does — so perfectly.

"I'm just tired. I started partying, by myself obviously, at 5am. Happy fucking Birthday to me!"

Mel smiled, although there was no happiness on her face. It was more a smile to cover the fact she knew I wasn't okay.

Damn it, Stacey. Keep your mouth shut!

I changed the topic and made a quick escape to the bathroom, attempting to compose myself before returning.

"I'll see you next week, yeah?"

Mel definitely knew I wasn't okay. The tone in her voice caught me off guard and I knew I had to convince her she would be seeing me next week.

"Yeah! Of course you will! See you Thursday!"

Back at home, I collapsed on the floor of the spare bedroom. Butcher's paper was plastered all over the floor and up the walls. Doodles covered nearly every inch and paint bottles, pencils, and sharpies were strewn everywhere. I missed my family. I missed my friends. I missed everything about what I once had. I hated that I had left and blamed myself for everything. I just wanted to wake up and the past three months would be some kind of horrible dream. Even though I'd be back in an abhorrent reality, I would prefer it over my present circumstances. Ian sent me a text message saying that he was going to pop around shortly, but when I heard his knock I was too drained to get up. I texted him that I would be home in a few hours, which is exactly how long it took me to get up off the floorboards. By the time Ian returned, I had sobered up enough to hold a conversation.

"Happy Birthday, Stace!"

He handed me a present and stood in the doorway as I unwrapped it. He couldn't stay long and insisted I open his gift. I held it in my hand, contemplating what was inside the neat wrapping. It felt like a box. Maybe chocolates? A book? Hopefully a memory-wiping drink that could make me forget everything that has happened this year... Or better yet, forget my entire life!

Maybe it's a 'Grow–Your–Own–Jesus'?

I turned the present over in my hands and listened while Ian began talking about God. I was slowly pulling up the corners of the wrapping as he was sharing about the Goodness of God. As I peeled back the paper, I suddenly realized what I was holding in my hands.

A Bible!

Ian got me a goddamn Bible.

"I know it says it's a teen version and you're quite mature for eighteen, but the lady at the store said it would be suitable for you!"

His face was warmed with a smile that reached from ear to ear. He chuckled with excitement that I now had my own bible. I wanted to ask him what the difference was between a teen version and a normal version but I didn't want to sound like an idiot.

I thought there was only one kind. Am I supposed to read every version?! I didn't even know how you were supposed to read it! Are you supposed to read it cover to cover in one sitting? For a long period of time like Ian always did every morning? Are there rules about reading it... can you read it 'wrong'?

I was still curious about God and Christianity and thought this was a really cool gift, but I was just worried I would go to hell if I read The Bible but still didn't fully believe in the guy it was about.

"The Book of Psalms is really great. You should have a go at reading some of that first!"

I had no idea what that meant, but nodded and thanked him for being so generous. I watched him drive away and stood in the door frame, clasping The Bible... wondering if sinners were even allowed to hold such a piece of literature. I didn't understand why it was so thick — maybe it contained the meaning of life? Or perhaps every Christian is crazy because of the amount of words they are required to read. I opened it and tried to find the 'Book of Psalms' Ian told me about. I read the first thing my eyes were drawn to... and gasped!

'Even if my father and mother abandon me, The Lord will hold me close.'

(Psalm 27:10 NLT)

What?! Why is that in there?! Not everyone's mum and dad leaves them! Does God know what has happened to me? Is this some kind of sick joke Ian is playing on me? Is this even a real Bible? How the fuck did that get in there? Why would that even be there? Is this supposed to make me think about going to church... because it certainly is causing me to contemplate the thought!

What would happen if I *did* go to church? What if God really was real and healed me of being sad? What if He took away all the painful stuff in my life, and everything became really awesome? Besides, if God was so good, then why did He let all the bad things happen to me? If He really was holding me close, why wasn't I aware of it?

Where was He when my innocence was taken?!

CHAPTER ELEVEN

I hadn't slept or eaten for three days. In case I ran out of time to compose letters to certain people, I had started writing notes on my phone. I turned off my password lock, planning to leave the notes app open so it would be the first thing someone found. I would down all the pills I had been stockpiling since leaving the shelter, with a bottle of vodka I was reserving for the occasion. I had an appointment with Mel at two o'clock, so I walked into town and stopped to have lunch at a café. Even though I freaked out eating in front of people and knew I would probably find myself in the nearest public toilet as soon as I finished the last bite... for some reason I was up for a challenge. I chose a café that was almost always deserted and ordered a sandwich, caramel milk shake and a Mars Bar slice.

Surrounded by silence, I focused on every mouthful. It took me more than half an hour to finish eating. By then, I was running the risk of being late to my appointment and I didn't want to raise any red flags by not showing up. I was stressing out because I wanted to purge straight away but resolved to as soon as I got home. I had to convince Mel I was okay. This could be problematic because she knew all the ways I lied.

A block away from Mel's office, 'Fix You' by Coldplay started playing. I wanted to compose a list of songs that could be played at my funeral, but hadn't had the chance yet. 'Fix You' was going to be on the top of the list. How ironic it happened to play when it did. A lot of the staff were away so the office building was quieter than usual. I sat in reception and wondered if this would be my last time here. Closing my eyes, I tried to pull myself together. I had forty minutes to reassure Mel I was hunky dory. Footsteps approached.

Breathe, Stacey... Breathe.

Mel always wore the most stunning outfits and had spectacular taste in shoes. She welcomed me with her warm, glowing smile. It was infectious... maybe it's a secret technique that therapists are taught to win you over with so you spill your deepest, darkest secrets.

"How has your week been?"

She closed the door behind her and I swallowed hard as I sat.

I can't fool her. I can't lie. Fuck. Mel, I'm not okay!!!

"Yeah, alright. Just the usual I guess."

Mel raised her eyebrow as if it was a cue to delve deeper into my response.

"How has your week been... really?"

After almost eighteen months of therapy, Mel witnessed me cry for the first time! I didn't want to cry and was trying my darndest to hide my emotions, but the tears would not stop falling! Resting my elbows on my knees, I hid my face.

"I knew you weren't fine the moment I saw you in reception. You weren't wearing your mask today. I think it's time to take that trip to hospital, darling."

"No, really I'm fine. It's okay. I'm just tired."

I didn't want to answer any of the questions that came my way, but for some reason I was giving Mel everything she wanted. The more I opened my mouth, the deeper the hole I dug. I was serving myself a one-way ticket to the hospital!

"I can't let you walk out those doors because I know you will do something stupid."

I couldn't even defend myself. I couldn't string together a pathetic lie to cover the truth. I turned my face from Mel and stared out the window. She made a few phone calls, trying to work out the best way to get me to hospital. We discussed the possibility of an ambulance, but both understood that wouldn't go down well. If I was off to hospital, there was no way in hell I was being made to go in a damn ambulance. Mel called Lindsay over and within ten minutes, she was at the office ready to take me. I felt like I was glued to the chair, my whole body paralyzed. Time seemed to stand still as I heard Mel and Lindsay chat, but my mind was zoning out and I couldn't understand clearly what they were saying. Everything was a blur.

Why are you doing this to me, Mel?! Why?!

By the time I finally got up to walk to Lindsay's car, I was sobbing. The trip to the hospital lasted thirty minutes and mercifully, by the time we parked, I had finally stopped crying. I had no idea what this process was going to be like.

What was going to happen to me? Was it actually going to be like 'Girl, Interrupted'? How long would I have to stay?

~

After waiting for two hours, I was finally called by a nurse to have a medical examination. Lindsay was still with me so I asked her to come along. Terrified, I didn't want to do any of this alone. My anxiety began to skyrocket as we followed the nurse to a spare room in Emergency. I lay on the bed as he went to get something. I didn't care what this examination entailed, but I really didn't want it done by a male! He placed odd sticky dots on my chest, checked my blood pressure, asked me questions, and then pointed to the scales.

Shit.

I instantly regretted eating so much before seeing Mel, especially because I didn't get the chance to purge. Lindsay was sitting right beside the scales and I didn't want her to see how fat I had allowed myself to become. I couldn't bring myself to look at the number but had to hide my distress. I was scared if they knew the truth about my relationship with food and my body image, they would force me into meal plans and therapy. That only meant losing control and becoming fat. And there was no way in hell I was going to do that! As I sat up on the bed, I looked at Lindsay. She was trying her best to remain happy and positive. A female nurse soon arrived and asked Lindsay to wait outside the curtain while she performed the next part of the examination. She asked me to strip down to my bra and undies, and although I wasn't fully naked, I had never felt so exposed in my life. The cuts on my wrist were nothing compared to the raised, pink, fleshy scars and large gashes covering much of my stomach. I held my breath as the nurse asked me to turn around so she could inspect every inch of me. The top of my thighs revealed deep, fleshy scars. The nurse asked how old the wounds were.

"You've got quite the decoration!"

If that was her attempt at making light of the situation, she was doing a terrible job. She checked the rest of my legs and scrutinized my stomach and arms. Surveying me up and down, she noted something on her clipboard and then looked at me, smirking.

"We're going to have to start calling you Chopper!"

Flipping the curtain open, she left me standing there, fumbling to pull my pants back up, reeling from what she had just said.

Who the fuck does she think she is?!

Thankfully Lindsay quickly closed the curtain, while I fixed my clothes. I sat back on the bed and waited for the male nurse to return. I couldn't believe what she had said. It was one thing to remark about the 'decorations', but calling me chopper? That was just completely uncalled for! I didn't mention a single word to Lindsay until we were taken back to a private waiting room. Someone else on staff came to inform us that the suicide prevention team (who would work out if I was at serious risk and actually needed to be admitted) were running late. He reviewed my situation and asked me further questions. I was giving him half-ass answers and down-played the severity. He asked Lindsay if there was anything she wanted to say or if there was anything they needed to be aware of.

"I think Stacey's pretty much covered most of it. Maybe just one thing that hasn't been addressed is her relationship with food and her body image."

Lindsay, shut up!!! If I was put on a meal plan, I was blaming her!

We had been at the hospital for four hours when Lindsay finally left. I felt bad she had stayed with me for so long. It was long past normal office hours and she had a family to return home to. She had gone above and beyond what I ever expected.

"I'll come see you tomorrow, okay? Make sure you tell them the truth!"

A security guard was called to stand at my door and make sure I didn't do a runner. I sat in the room alone, waiting for someone, anyone, to come and talk to me. I was beginning to question my own sanity. I felt like a proper crazy person... being interrogated, called Chopper, guarded by my own security, and now trapped in a small room. If the psych ward was anything like this, I did NOT want to be admitted!

A man with an aura of smoke arrived at 9.15pm. He looked more miserable than I felt. He studied me further and did a splendid job at making me feel like crap. My patience was wearing thin and the thought of a bed, even if it was on the psych ward, sounded inviting.

"Look at you. You're young. You're beautiful... You really don't want to kill yourself, do you?"

Don't tell me what I do and don't want to do, mate.

"Umm, yeah. I do. I actually do want to die."

He asked me more questions before stepping outside to make a phone call. I closed my eyes and tried to muster up the energy to be brave. The security guard was still standing outside. I wondered what would happen if I locked myself in the bathroom adjacent to the room. I had already burrowed a hole bigger than I could wriggle out of and decided it wasn't wise to make it any worse.

"We might not have any beds for you tonight. What if we organize you to start counselling in a couple of days? I can arrange for you to see someone tomorrow, and we'll go from there?"

I was perfectly okay with Lindsay and Mel being my professional support system. Well, I was far from being perfectly okay, but I absolutely did not want anyone else rooting through my mess! I was a handful to work with, and getting through all my walls had to be a monumental task. I didn't want even more professionals spotlighting around my personal spaces. I was happy with Mel and Lindsay, thanks.

Tell him the truth... Remember what Lindsay said... tell him the truth!!

"Look... if I don't get a bed here tonight, I'll be back in a few days... except they will be rushing me in on a stretcher because of a suicide attempt. But, I mean, it's up to you guys."

The words capsized out before I could even process them. The man straightened his posture, excused himself from the room and made another phone call. I could hear everything he was saying, and it made me laugh. Lindsay would be so proud!

"Yeah look mate, I have an eighteen-year-old female here. She says if we don't give her a bed tonight she'll go home and kill herself... I'll bring her up now... Right-o mate."

The stretch to the psych ward was the longest of my life! We made so many turns down deserted hallways. At the end, there were only two places to turn — the children's ward or the psych ward. It had only just clocked over 10pm when I arrived. I was greeted by three sets of eyes trailing my every move as I hovered outside the nurse's station. I waited on a seat and observed the nurses on duty gather around the suicide prevention man. My bag was confiscated — something about removing hazardous objects or items I could use to harm myself. Lindsay had mentioned they could take my shoelaces, but they didn't. Obviously they weren't doing a stellar job at confiscating hazardous objects. The curious eyes had shifted closer. Apparently I was more interesting than the television.

"New girl! New girl!! We have a new girl!!!"

Oh god, fucking shoot me now!.

A man, who looked to be in his forties, was jumping up and down. He was wearing a dressing gown and pointing me out to the other two men in the room. He started walking toward me but thankfully a nurse came to my rescue and guided me to my room.

The room had four beds, all of which were empty. I took the one opposite the door with a window looking out to a garden area. There was a desk/wardrobe combination piece that provided a makeshift wall between the other beds, granting a little privacy. The nurse handed me a cup of water accompanied by a tablet I apparently needed before bed. She then went to go and find the nurse assigned to me until the shift change later the next morning. I didn't want to take the tablet. I also didn't want to see what would happen if you argued with the nurses. I was sitting at the desk when my nurse walked back in. She knocked on the side of the wardrobe. Everyone else I had to see today had either been horrible or looked horrible. This nurse was young and friendly.

What a pleasant change.

She sat on my bed and started chatting. She could tell I was upset and scared but she treated me normally — something every other nurse at the hospital had failed to do. She handed over my bag and informed me there was a '*No Electronics*' policy on the ward.

"What about music? Can I listen to music?"

"Unfortunately no. I'm sorry"

There is no fucking way I'm going to be stuck in this loony bin without my music!! MEL!! What have you done?!

If anyone had told me about this policy I wouldn't have been as honest about my need for a bed. However because my nurse seemed ten times kinder than the others, I didn't have the guts to bitch at her. She filled me in on more of the rules and daily routine of the ward: the nurses, activities and night checks.

"You'll probably see a light shine in the room every hour but that's just us making sure you're okay!"

Three months ago, when I left home, my life had been thrown into limbo... but this? Now I had no idea what was going to happen next! I didn't know how long I would be here. I didn't know what kind of drugs they would try to pump in to me. I'm just suicidal, not psychotic!! My mental illness isn't as bad as the three people I've seen already.

I'm a smart kid... I've just had a rough time. I don't belong here!!!

CHAPTER TWELVE

The tablet I was given turned out to be a knock-you-out-to-the-world sleeping pill! I basically passed out and didn't wake again until a nurse informed me breakfast was ready. I blinked at the sliver of daylight between the curtains. I had no idea what time it was nor any intention of leaving my bed. My nurse from last night was still on shift and settled down at my desk.

"Did you want to come and eat some brekkie?"

I sat up and stretched. Those tablets were good stuff! I couldn't even remember the last time I had such a good sleep. She stayed around for a while and reminded me of everything she told me last night. She said I didn't have to participate if I didn't want, but socializing would help make the time go faster. She accompanied me to the common area and explained how meal times worked. There were people wandering around but thankfully only three people were still at the table. An elderly woman was sitting in a lounge chair about five meters from where I sat. She was wearing sunglasses and swearing at everyone who walked past. I didn't know if the three people at the table were unstable, so I didn't acknowledge them. Looking straight down at my food tray, I tediously spread vegemite over my toast. As I took a bite, I glanced up to see someone staring at me. Her eyes were wide and her smile almost too big for her face. She told me she believed in aliens — and she was getting discharged. The guy beside her seemed normal, although he hadn't opened his mouth yet... so I didn't hold high expectations.

I don't belong here.

I!

DON'T!

FUCKING!

BELONG!

HERE!!!

After I finished eating breakfast, I went straight back to my room, and stayed there until Lindsay came to visit about an hour later.

"How's it going?"

I didn't want to hang on the ward, so we found an empty cafeteria to talk. She brought me chocolate bars in an attempt to cheer me up.

Oh, fucking brilliant!

"You need rest though. This is where you need to be."

I need rest? You mean rest from my whole LIFE! Being in this place isn't going to help with anything!

"Shit! I had an appointment with the sexual abuse place today! Ugh!"

For once in my life, I wished I could attend this appointment. As much as I didn't want to dredge up that horror, I would prefer that appointment than spend another minute in hospital. I had been on a waiting list for weeks, and now the day had finally arrived I was trapped — here! Great!

"It's okay. Ring them when you are discharged. They will understand. Don't worry."

Yeah, understand that I'm fucking mentally unstable!

I wanted Lindsay to smuggle me away with her. She promised if I persisted for the weekend, she would come see me again on Monday, and we could talk through my exit plan and make sure I was in a healthy headspace. *MONDAY?* It was only Friday morning!

There is no way I'm going to stay in here that long!

"How are things going?"

I was outside the nurse's station with my back to everyone in the lounge room. There was so much going on. I guess the nurse was right: socializing made time pass faster. I'm sure I was the only person on the ward who thought being a recluse in their room was the best option. Why sit out with everyone else, when you could hate life just as much on your own. I was mad Mel had sent me here.

Doesn't she know how traumatizing it is to be surrounded by all these nut jobs?!

"It's nothing like *'Girl, Interrupted.'*"

I had called Mel and was airing out how the whole ordeal wouldn't be so bad if I was able to listen to my music. One of the nurses said there was a CD player I could use, but who the hell even owns CD's anymore? The phone was next to a computer in the corner of the room, and a guy was annoyed that a nurse made him move so I could have some privacy. He repositioned himself closer, hinting that he wanted to get back on the computer.

"I'm so sorry, darling."

I wish I hadn't let my mask slip. I wish I hadn't listened to Lindsay when she said to be honest. I wish I had just shut up and quietly killed myself. If I ever escape this nightmare, I know what not to do next time! There is no way I am coming back here alive.

"Hopefully I'll be out by Monday. I hate it here, Mel. Everyone is so... weird."

I knew if I didn't successfully kill myself, I would end up just like these people. I would be the twenty-five year old who believed in aliens... Or, the thirty-two year old whose young kids came to visit every weekend. Perhaps I would be the fifty year old stuck in the mind of her once vibrant teenage self. Or even the seventy year old swearing at everyone walking by. I would live the rest of my life being addicted to Valium, relying on anti-depressants to drag me out of bed and having more therapy sessions during the week than social outings!

"Look, I'm going to go because there's this freak wanting to use the computer. I'll let you know what happens."

I didn't want to hang up. I thought about staying on the phone and speaking with Mel until the nurses forced me to hang up. I wanted her to come and rescue me. Couldn't she wave her magic wand? Anything rather than being stuck in this hellhole of a psycho-house!!

My new nurse came around not long after her shift had started. I presume I was the only patient who wasn't hanging in the living area. I was more upset than when I was first admitted and I'm sure I looked like hell. A despairingly lethal cocktail of angry, sad, scared and annoyed was pressing in on every inch of me.

"Do you reckon I'll be able to go home tomorrow?"

She didn't commit to anything, but did say she would organize for me to see the doctor in the morning. Apparently it was rare for someone to leave on the weekend. Was I supposed to back down and feel sorry for the doctor who had to come in to assess me? Was I supposed to tell her not to worry... that I was happy to stay longer... just to make the doctor's life more comfortable? I didn't care if the doctor was flying in from another state! I want to be assessed and discharged as soon as possible! I didn't care what day or time it was...

"How do you think you will cope if you leave this weekend? Do you think staying for, say... a week, will be better?"

Fuck off!!!

"To be honest, this place is so disturbing..."

At least I was honest with one thing!

"... but I think I will be fine if I leave. Being in here has really made me re-evaluate everything. Life is so precious, and I'm still so young!"

The nurse wasn't fazed by my obvious sarcasm and reassured me that she would organize the doctor for the morning. She made certain I understood the chances of being released weren't great and that the doctor would probably send me back to the ward. As we were speaking, an elderly lady was brought into the room. She was probably late sixties and shuffled in behind the nurses to the bed closest to the door. I could hear her tell one of the nurses something about the last time she was here.

Last time? Oh great, I'm sharing a room with a bat-shit crazy old lady!

My nurse moved to distract me and asked how I was finding my stay. Why would I like being in hospital, surrounded by random strangers who are freaking me out? Was this supposed to be some kind of life-altering experience that would somehow change me? Was she after practical feedback that would ensure I didn't return like the patient who just entered the room?

"It's scary, but I know it's where I need to be."

I saw the light of the torch flash through the door every hour. I couldn't sleep, not only because I felt sick at the thought of staying longer, but because my new roomie was snoring and murmuring about her dead brother in her sleep. I was worried that if I called for the nurse, they would give me more sleeping pills and I didn't want to be completely wiped out. I mean, who knew what the old lady was capable of? What if she stood at the end of my bed without me knowing? What if she went through my bag? I lay on my back, listening to every rise and fall of her chest, every sigh, groan and mutter. I chewed over what my nurse said regarding my chances of being discharged. I felt so out of touch with reality.

Not having music was driving me more insane than I was two days ago! Overhearing conversations during the day — and the deathly quiet of night was harrowing. My thoughts started to drift off. Maybe it was the insomnia or boredom that caused me to start pondering the idea of God. It had been one month since I left the shelter... one week since I received the Bible from Ian. If God was real, then why did He let me end up in a psych ward? Even if He existed, there was no way He could love someone like me. Georgina and Ian had told me God loved everyone, but when you are physically and mentally bruised and scared... this concept is seriously impossible to wrap your head around. If God knew about everything that happened and all that was still to happen, then why did He allow me to be born into the family I was?

The dawn's rays were seeping through the curtain. I hadn't slept a single wink. The elderly lady woke up, finally done with her snoring and sleep talking. The entire ward became a hub of busyness. Morning time was always interesting. I pulled the blankets over my head and took a deep breath.

Please just let me disappear.

I heard the food trolley roll in, and feet hustling to grab their tray. Each mealtime you would think some of these people hadn't eaten for months! I had no intention of leaving my room until I saw the doctor later that morning.

"Good morning, Stacey!"

Why were the nurses so chatty every morning? I knew she was going to try and talk me into eating breakfast. I had only eaten breakfast since being admitted Thursday night. It was now Saturday morning.

"Come and have some brekkie while you wait for the doctor. He should only be another hour or so!"

I declined her offer which didn't seem to surprise her. I mentioned I hadn't sleep very well during the night and just wanted some quiet time before seeing the doctor. At least all my nurses on the ward were ten times better than nurse "chopper." The morning was really quite beautiful and I wished I was outside enjoying it — without a stupid hospital band around my wrist. I sat at the desk staring at the sky. It was the most glorious shade of blue I had ever seen! It almost looked fluorescent, yet it was soft and warm on the eyes. Clouds are my favorite thing in nature and they were perfectly placed — with sculptured, fluffy edges. I wished I could lie on one and spy on the world below. I was captivated by a sense of peace that flooded me.

Breathe. It's all going to be okay. Breathe. Breathe.

My mind suddenly became less jumbled. All the demanding thoughts that had consumed every second, seemed to cease.

God, I don't know if You can hear me... and I don't know if You want to hear me... but pleeease let me be discharged. I promise if I leave today I will come to church with Georgina. I really will. I promise. Please.

CHAPTER THIRTEEN

Maybe the universe dealt me a good card or maybe God really did hear me! Either way, I was discharged on Sunday... and now a week later, I found myself on the way to the place I never thought I would find myself: church! Georgina told me the people wouldn't be weird:

"They are just people... like you." I couldn't picture hundreds of people like me: depressed, alcoholic, abused, broken.

She's just saying that to make me feel better.

I followed her through the front door. There were two people on either side who greeted us. Everyone was smiling from ear to ear. No amount of vodka or weed could make me be that happy!

George, this is already fucking weird!

We walked in to a big room with a stage up front. There were rows of chairs, but not the wooden pews I expected. People were moving toward the front of the stage as we sat in the second row.

"Remember you don't have to do anything. Just take it all in and have fun!"

Suddenly about twenty people swarmed the front as several people walked onto stage and started playing music. If I didn't know they were about to sing God songs, I would have thought this was a mini concert! I stood watching the people in front of me. They were jumping up and down in a mosh pit, clapping their hands and yelling at the top of their lungs... They didn't care about how they looked! Feeling over-whelmed, I tried to focus on the person in front of me. She was wearing a wide brim hat. *I thought it was a sin to wear hats inside? Especially in church!* It was going to be a loooong morning! A lady on stage, who was called a Pastor (although she didn't wear a flowing white robe), asked if there were any new people. The girl in the wide brimmed hat turned around and smiled at me. Georgina raised her hand and pointed me out to everyone.

Did they do this so they knew who the sinners were and to stay away from them? Were they highlighting who needed an exorcism? Maybe this was warning the parents to keep their children clear? Hello... yes, it is I! A dirty sinner, coming to corrupt you all and make you feel uncomfortable with my sin-filled life that I love so much!

I didn't want everyone to know I was "new"... although I'm sure all Christians have some kind of radar that can pick up a sinner within a ten-kilometer radius. Another Pastor (who also wasn't wearing a robe), walked on stage and started to preach — a term I learnt means "to speak"... Christians and their stupid slang! The more I listened to the conversations around me, the more I learnt that these people had their own language.

"So good": That was great. Commonly used approximately ten times in one minute.

"Preach": Not to be mistaken with when someone is speaking on stage... Use this when you agree with someone!

"So love/d": Christians love everything, apparently. They love everything SO much! So, sooo much!

"C'mon": Not to be confused with Leyton Hewitt (although probably meaning the same thing), this is their second favorite word and is used the most after "so good"

It's obnoxious. They're all fucking obnoxious.

Remarkably, I started feeling the same great sense of peace as when I watched the sky last week at hospital. I slowed my breathing down and tried to work out what was going on. There were a hundred tiny butterflies inside my stomach, dancing to a beautiful melody I couldn't hear. It was as if electricity was flowing through my veins causing the corners of my mouth to widen.

Holy shit!!! Am I being brain washed?!

I tried to zone out the Pastor... just in case his words *were* perfectly chosen for the purpose of brain washing. I centered back on the girl with the wide brim hat. Everyone in the front row was intently engaged, occasionally yelling encouragement as the Pastor preached. How rude! Surely, *Thou shall not interrupt a Pastor* was a commandment?

My attempt to not listen, failed. It was as if everything he was saying was exactly what I needed. It was as though his words were the key that fitted perfectly into my heart and made everything right. I started to feel more at peace with each word. I looked over to Georgina. Like the rest of the crazy Christians in the front row, she was watching the Pastor intently.

Who was this guy? And why was everyone fixated on what he was saying? Why was I so fixated?

The service finished with a song and I found myself standing and tapping my feet along to the beat. I didn't understand why people were raising their hands. Did they think God was going to hand them a gift or something? They looked ridiculous... but it was inexplicably comforting. The song soon finished and the room erupted in applause. I clapped too, but because the singers had talent... even though I didn't understand a single thing they were singing. People milled back to their seats and started to leave. No one looked unhappy. Not a single face was washed with sadness. There were no defeated or downcast eyes. The only time I ever saw this many upbeat people was in a room full of drunks... and these people around me certainly weren't under the influence. Their energy was contagious; and as I watched each person smiling generously, I also began to smile.

"I want to introduce you to someone..."

I followed Georgina as she weaved around more smiling groups of people to the front. There were a group of people standing in a line wearing nametags. They too, were smiling.

"Stacey, this is Paula... Paula, Stacey!"

Paula smiled as I mirrored her uncomfortably.

Why did George want me to meet her? Is she the one that brain washes people? Shit... is this where the exorcisms take place?

Paula looked me in the eyes, as if she was reading my every thought.

Who the hell is this lady? Is she the woman version of Jesus?

Everything I was feeling during the service almost doubled as Paula began talking to me. She asked me how I liked the service before drifting in to a conversation about God and my background with religion.

"Have you asked Jesus into your heart?"

Were Jesus and God the same thing? And why the hell would you have them in your heart?

I shook my head, unable to form any words. Georgina was by my side and I sincerely hoped she wouldn't leave. I wasn't scared or overwhelmed anymore... I just didn't want to be alone, and Georgina was all I had. If she left, I was out of here!

"Do you want to ask Him into your heart?"

Without thinking through what Paula said, my head nodded in agreement. It was as if I wasn't in control of my own movements! My mouth was speaking and agreeing to things before I could think what to say.

I glanced at Georgina.

"Yay!"

Yay? Fucking yay? What is going on?! Why am I feeling so okay with this? Why does my body know what to do? Why does my heart feel so at peace with whatever is going on? Georgina... why 'yay'?!

She gently placed her hand on my back, muttering the words "so good," which, by now, I was convinced was some kind of

Christian mantra! Paula asked me to repeat what she was saying, and I willingly agreed. With every phrase, my entire body felt lighter. I almost felt like bursting out in laughter - not because I felt stupid, but because there was an overwhelming sense of joy beginning to wash over me. An unprecedented sense of euphoria, that seemed to appear out of nowhere. After I recited the last word, Paula then asked if I wanted to be baptized with the Holy Spirit.

If it's as good of a spirit as vodka... then yes! Yes please!

Again, I nodded my head before I even had the chance to fully process what was being said. I soon learnt that God, Jesus and The Holy Spirit are the same. God is the guy in the sky, Jesus is the man who walked the earth and died on the cross, and the Holy Spirit is the one who apparently helps guide us through every day. I was confused, but knew Georgina would help me understand it better.

"You'll probably start speaking in a different language. We call it our Heavenly Language. It makes absolutely no sense to us, but God knows exactly what is being said! It's our spirit talking with Heaven!"

This is so weird... why am I not feeling strange about it all? Different language? I took Indonesian and French lessons at school... and I'm not fluent in either one. I know the French terms for 'umbrella' and 'cow', but I can't repeat those two words over and over again. Maybe I could count to fifty in Indonesian really fast so it sounds like a sentence.

"I don't know any other language... at least not fluently."

Georgina and Paula chuckled, as if I was joking, but seri-ously... what the hell was this Heavenly Language?

"That's okay! You won't know what you're saying. Words will come to you... just say what ever comes. It's okay!"

I looked at Georgina for reassurance. Her smile was bigger than it had been all morning.

"What if nothing happens? I mean, like, what if no words come out?"

"They will... just trust!"

Trust what?! What the fuck am I supposed to be trusting here, Paula?!?!!

Once again, Paula and Georgina put their hands on me and started to pray. I had no idea what they were saying, mainly be-cause they were both going in and out of some weird language... their Heavenly Language, I guess. I began to get caught up in what I was feeling. The butterflies were back, and my head was spinning; but not in a *'I-want-to-pass-out-from-all-the-weird bullshit-that-I've-seen-this-morning'* kind of way. I felt oddly comforted by something, I wasn't quite sure what it was. Maybe it's God?

Is it God??? So good, c'mon. Shit! What am I doing?! I don't know how to speak Christian!!!

I felt so at peace, as if I was sitting by a river, or lying in an open lush field. Everything around me became a blur; and be-fore I knew it, I began speaking another language...

CHAPTER FOURTEEN

Signed, sealed and delivered... I am now a Christian! Well, I don't actually know if saying a few words and speaking some kind of gibberish makes me a Christian... who knows!

I lay on my lounge room floor trying to process all that had transpired that morning. I still felt such a great sense of peace with a unique joy bubbling through! I had never felt like this before. It was different to the calm sensation of being high and a far better buzz than my red baby gave me. Although I had been out of hospital a week, I had been sleeping back at the shelter — mainly for my own protection. Lindsay and Mel didn't think it would be wise to let me live by myself. They thought I would overdose if I were alone. The doctors thought that too. I was only prescribed five tablets of medication at a time, so when I run out I had to return to the chemist to order the next five. It was another way of keeping tabs on me. I hated it! I opened the Bible to where I found the verse about my parents. Flicking through several pages, my eyes stumbled upon something else that made me sigh.

'Now I will take the load from your shoulders; I will free your hands from their heavy tasks.'

(Psalm 81:6 NLT)

I had no idea how this whole God-thing worked, but if Ian was healed of MS and I was discharged from the hospital — despite the nurse's doubtfulness — then surely God could take the load from my shoulders, right? If it was written in The Bible, then it had to be true!

My hands were heavy from holding together the shattered remains of my broken heart... they were weary from wiping the tears every night. This load was far too burdensome for me to carry anymore. If God could take even the smallest weight I had been forced to carry, then I was more than happy to follow Him and be a Christian. Paula said that the Heavenly Language was really important and I should take some time to speak it during the week. Apparently it helped strengthen our relationship with God. Religion and Relationship are two different things and the church I went to with Georgina wasn't a fan of religion... maybe that's why I felt okay to attend! Relationships I can do, though quite badly, but I can do them!

Every emotion from my experience that morning was still present and as I sat in bed, they began to intensify. I was flipping through the Bible, trying to figure out the proper way to read it, when I suddenly broke out in a chant of my Heavenly Language. My eyes closed and I began feeling as though I were floating.

WHAT IS HAPPENING?!?!

My body started to shake, almost like I were convulsing. Surprisingly though, I remained at peace and full of joy! I felt as if the chains wrapped around me were being broken as I shook. My Heavenly Language became thicker. I felt like I was floating higher. This was more intense than any drug trip I had ever experienced!! Sometime later, when I finally opened my eyes, I felt odd... in a good way. I felt free, as if my insides had been cleansed and my brain recharged. It was as if my eyes were washed clean. Maybe this was how God worked? Maybe He literally *did* take something off me — liberating me from the heaviness I was carrying!

Shit...

Emotions! I was feeling such an array of emotions since becoming a Christian. I cried (in front of people!) and felt things I assume a normal person experiences on a regular basis. I was no longer in a constant state of numbness... and it was weird. I didn't expect my life to radically change the moment I became a Christian, in fact, it was still messed up. I still hated myself, but I didn't want to die anymore. It felt like I was on a vacation... but vacations always come to an end.

It's just a matter of time before all this joy and wonder comes crumbling down, and I'm back to square one.

Overwhelmed, I grabbed a bottle of Vodka and lay on the couch. I didn't want to 'encounter' the Holy Spirit tonight, nor did I want to be in a good mood. I just wanted to feel like the old me. Had I dived straight in to the deep end and waved goodbye to my old self too quickly? I broke the seal and swallowed a big mouthful. I clenched my teeth as the liquid ran down my throat, warming my belly and opening the door to a night of forgetting. Almost half the bottle had disappeared. I stumbled from the couch to the middle of the room and fell on the floor.

"God, you're so stupid!"

I was scorning at my pathetic life as I began conversing with the One Whom, only a few weeks ago, I had fallen head-over-heels for. He can't be mad at my bitterness and using my drunk state to heatedly call Him out.

"You were never there for me, God... dude! You let my life get fucked up. You sat back and didn't do a damn thing. Shame on you!"

I erupted in a fit of laughter. I tilted the bottle and continued drinking as I listened to the darkest punk/rock/metal music on my phone.

"Do you even Love me?! Huh?! Bet You don't! Bet You're just like them! Picture-perfect-bullshit... but behind closed doors... HA! You know exactly what happened! And what did You do?! NOTHING!!!"

Lurching to my feet, I jumped around the lounge room, screaming along with the music at the top of my lungs. The good thing about living in such a low socioeconomic neighborhood is that everyone is used to loud, drunk people. I started spinning in a circle — bottle still clenched. I kept drinking, kept swirling. Drinking and swirling. Swirling and drinking. I'm happy when I'm either high or drunk. I'm ecstatic when I'm both.

I don't care how amazing this Jesus thing may be... I'm never giving up what makes me forget the hell I've endured. Christians don't get my kind of life. Nobody gets this life. Hell, I don't even get this life!

I collapsed to the floor in a dizzy, joyful state. My Bible was sitting right where I fell. What a coincidence! Flicking through the pages, I was still screaming the lyrics of my favorite "I-hate-the-world, fuck-you!" songs. I stopped flipping and landed straight on the same page I turned to the very first time I opened it.

'Even if my father and mother abandon me, the LORD will
hold me close.'

(Psalm 27:10 NLT)

I flung the Bible across the room.

"FUCK YOU!"

I downed the remaining vodka and tossed the bottle across
the room, too. I started crying again... something I had been doing nonstop since becoming a Christian. But this time, in all my
drunken glory, I was crying because I was frustrated. Furious
this verse kept popping up, I was mad I couldn't understand or
come to terms with it.

When your own blood doesn't want you, you can't expect *anyone* to.

CHAPTER FIFTEEN

66 Based on that declaration of faith, I baptize you in the name of the Father, the Son and the Holy Spirit."

I was clenching Paula's hand so tight I thought her circulation was going to cut off. Water baptism was something I wanted to do, but I was terrified of getting dunked underwater. I was deeply convinced the events over the past two months were not random, but in fact God-ordained appointments. I hadn't cut or purged since becoming a Christian, and as far as everyone was concerned, I was doing great. Behind closed doors however, was another story. I was drinking every night and restricting my food intake. Even though getting baptized was something I wanted for myself, I also thought I would gain more approval and praise from my new friends. The entire church building was packed. Unlike every other person getting baptized before me, I didn't have any family members standing beside me. There were only three people with me who I had known for only a couple of months... and that seriously made me feel like shit. I hated being reminded how messed-up my life was. On a morning that was supposed to be full of celebration and exciting new beginnings, all I could think about was how I hurt.

Is this what the rest of my life will be like? Surrounded by other happy families, while struggling to accept it?

I let go of Paula's hand and locked on to the Pastor baptizing me. I knew within seconds I would be under water.

Breathe... It's just a few seconds and you'll be up again. Breathe...

I was so focused on my breathing I became oblivious to my surroundings. For a moment I didn't care that my family wasn't there, or that I was afraid of water. I felt at peace...and calm! I was soon immersed in water and a strange sense of euphoria. I thought I would be freaking out. I had almost drowned after being held under water a few years ago, and feared the memory of that day would completely overtake everything... but I was serene. It felt like I was under the water for five minutes (although it was probably only a few seconds!) I have never been able to open my eyes under water, yet here I was — eyes wide open. I could see the distorted reflections of people above me, an abstract watercolor masterpiece. I could hear this beautiful melody being played. I assumed it was coming from the band on stage, however I hadn't heard anything beforehand. I didn't want to be brought back to the surface. I wanted to remain submerged, wrapped in peace, listening to that beautiful melody.

My feet hit the cold wooden floor and steered me to the cupboard where my vodka bottles were lined perfectly like soldiers. I was still half asleep but functioning as if I was wide-awake. I cradled all six bottles toward the bathroom. It hadn't been 24 hours since I was baptized...

Could something weird be happening like the night I was baptized in the Holy Spirit?

I placed all the bottles on the bathroom counter and paused. Pouring vodka down the sink was the last thing I would willingly do. I picked up one of the bottles and slowly screwed the cap off.

Why was I doing this?

"I now have a Spirit Who is much stronger than you. I don't need you anymore. You no longer control me."

I began speaking my Heavenly Language as I drained every single drop down the sink. In stunned silence, I contemplated the now empty bottles. What just happened wasn't my own doing. Ordinarily, it took at least thirty minutes to wake in the morning, and there's no way I would ever jump out of bed to spill my precious red baby down the sink. This was in no way a work of my own flesh. It *had* to be the Spirit Who now lived inside me. I knew it was a God thing... there's no other explanation!

I'm an alcoholic for crying out loud... This is impossible for me to do! I can't go a single day without drinking — and I just drained every single drop of alcohol in my house down the bathroom sink!

I threw the empty bottles in the recycling bin, and then lay on the floor. Normally, I find myself sprawled out during some of the hardest anxiety attacks, sadness and feelings of worthlessness. Yet, something about being lower seemed unusually comforting to me. I was actually on top of the world, which made descending to the floor even more bizarre. I stared at the ceiling as a smile tickled across my cheeks. For a moment, I wasn't remembering the negative things I was still doing and how I was concerned about how they might cancel every positive step forward. Rather, I was blissfully engrossed in the goodness of what just happened. Vodka had been my escape. It aided me out of my bedroom and onto the school bus. It helped keep the mask secure. It was the reason I could endure such horrendous treatment. It numbed me, comforted me, and made me forget. I could always rely on it, no matter how my day was going... It was my constant: where my morning would begin, and my evening close.

What's going to happen now I've thrown my support system down the sink? Of course I can easily go and buy some more... maybe that's my first agenda for tomorrow. If I don't drink, I will have to cut. And if I don't drink or cut, I'll definitely have to restrict and purge big time! God, what are You doing?! I don't have the strength to follow through with this.

Everyone at church would be thrilled once they found out I had poured my alcohol down the sink. Lindsay and Mel would be stoked, too. I was happy as well... but the more I started to ponder on what happened, the more I began to question God and fear what was around the corner.

Somehow I had worked my way up to being four months self-harm free and almost one month of sobriety... yet to be honest, I was worse than ever. I was still seeing Lindsay and Mel frequently, but wearing my mask (as well as my newfound faith) to bullshit how well I was coping with life. Even though I had no desire to drink vodka (in fact the thought of it started to make me feel sick), the compulsion to control my weight was cascading out of control. Weighing myself twice a day, I was purging at least three times daily and becoming trapped in unimaginable cycles of binge/purge. I hadn't eaten for three days and was bone-weary from a full day at work. I had decided to resign the following week because I couldn't take the stress of being in the same town as my parents. As much as I dearly loved my boss and co-workers, I couldn't put myself through the mental strain anymore. I knew my boss would be gutted, but she was one of the greatest people I had ever met and was aware of how difficult things had been for me. She would understand and wish the best for me.

I convinced myself that eating dinner would be fine. I walked to the kitchen, my body aching from lack of nutrition and exhaustion. I never stored more than two meals in my cupboards and decided to cook a bowl of rice. Perched on the kitchen floor, I watched the microwave timer count down.

Eat this and you will be fine. Breathe...

I placed three spoons of rice in a bowl, settled on the couch, and stirred the spoon around the bowl until I worked up the courage to take the first mouthful. I knew eating was the right thing to do but I couldn't get over the feeling of disgust. Disappointed I still had a few kilos to go until I hit my goal weight, I was deathly afraid that one meal would cause me to instantly gain weight. I finally put the spoon to my mouth and swallowed.

Instant regret!

I threw the bowl across the floor and ran to the bathroom.

One mouthful! One goddamn mouthful was all it took to break me.

I assumed my customary position at the toilet bowl and heaved up the rice.

Fat bitch! What were you thinking?!

There was nothing else in my stomach except water, so the purge was pathetic. I predicted I would soon binge again, possibly within a week, and then that would possibly send me down a spiral of intense self-loathing and cutting. I sighed against the bathtub and quietly cried. I felt as though I was being suffocated by a homegrown fat suit. Even though people were quick to tell me I wasn't fat... I felt fat. I saw fat.

I am fat.

I stared at my hands, red and sore from purging.

Even your fingers are fat! You disgusting pig!

I wanted to carve every inch of fat from my body... to slice the layers away until I was my goal weight, and then keep slivering until I wasn't fat anymore. I was always sporting the same kind of outfit because I was repulsed by how I looked. Jeans, a baggy top and cardigan... no matter how hot.

People don't want to see my fat rolls in a tight fitting t-shirt. Nobody wants to see my pudgy arms on display. If I'm revolted by how I look, then others sure-as-hell are, too.

My stomach growled, so I lay on the bathroom floor in an attempt to ease the discomfort. I was in so much pain due to treating my body poorly, but that wasn't going to stop me from reaching my goal weight. Nobody's wise words could convince me to stop hurting myself. Until I could view every bone in my body, nobody could stop me. The only thing I liked about myself were my eyes... although when I thought more deeply about that, I begin to despise them too. They had seen way too many obscenities... too much destruction.

I couldn't move off the bathroom floor because my body was cramped up and I didn't have any energy to stand. The moon brightened the night and filled the bathroom window.

God, I can't do this anymore.

CHAPTER SIXTEEN

I wanted to tell Mel the truth. I sat in her office staring at her, hoping she would be able to look through my mask and decipher what was going on without me having to utter a single word. Paula was the only person who knew most of my current status, but I hadn't disclosed the complete story. I wanted to be totally honest with Mel, but I was petrified she would send me back to hospital. Even though I didn't think I was in a state of meltdown, I wasn't sure what parameters were deemed 'at risk'. I knew not to be as obvious as to indicate suicidal tendencies. Right now, I didn't really want to die. But I wasn't coping well. Paula approached everything with prayer and biblical wisdom that was practical — exactly what I needed, but I still wanted Mel to know all that was going on inside me, not just what I was filtering to her. I didn't want to hear, "God has your back" or, "He is making all things new." I yearned to get to the bottom of the deeply-rooted emotional pain making me feel so worthless: disgusting, unlovable, pathetic.

I suspected I wasn't processing things like a normal person and it was driving me insane. Terrorized by any sudden movement around me, I always had the sense something bad could happen at any moment. There were still days I couldn't get out of bed because depression held me captive between the blankets. I struggled with anxiety attacks, making it near impossible to leave the house. My sleep was tormented by nightmares about my childhood, and I thought I would wake to see my parents. I was a teenager, yet completely terrified of everything. I am an absolute mess and I can't seem to improve my life in the slightest... no matter how hard I may try.

"How have things been?"

Mel... please help me!

My eyes darted around the office as I desperately tried to express one of the hundreds of thoughts galloping through my mind. I wanted to offload how I thought nobody could ever love me... not just in a physical sense but also romantically. I wanted her to know how complex this issue was for me now that I'm a Christian. I believed in sexual purity and all the ways it played out in our lives. But I couldn't grasp the concept of purity after losing my innocence at such a young age... by someone who wasn't supposed to hurt me like that. I couldn't understand how God could let such evil rob me of my childhood and destroy my future. I wanted to talk about how there was only one guy I had ever let in close, yet I gave over something precious despite the fact I didn't want to.

I wanted her to know how difficult life was for me.

...And messy!

...And how absolutely shattered and scattered I felt.

"Yeah, good! This year is off to a great start!"

I smiled, anticipating her to call me out on my bullshit... but she didn't. She quietly waited for me to elaborate why this year was off to a great start. I had nothing to say.

The only thing I'm not doing is drinking, which I can't justify celebrating because I've fallen off the wagon with everything else. My life feels like a broken record, constantly repeating the same cycle over and over again!

Becoming a Christian was definitely the best thing I have ever done, but believing in God didn't make my life magically better. There were still more bad days than good, which was so disheartening. I had no idea what to do, nor the strength to do anything I suspected I should be doing. Life was exhausting, and with every new day I was more convinced death was the only way to interrupt the cycle. I wondered what Mel was writing on her notepad as I stared out the window, watching people walk past. I so desperately wanted to be them. Anyone other than myself.

"How are you going with eating?"

I'm still fat, aren't I?

"Ehh, still the same, I guess. Nothing much has changed. Just the same ol' same ol' messed up Stacey."

I ran my fingers over my knuckles and wrist bone. I knew Mel didn't specialize in eating disorders, so there wasn't much she could say to me other than recommend I see an ED specialist. She could try to talk to me about my feelings around eating and maybe that would allow us to discuss the more deeply-rooted issues. However, Mel knew I hated talking about feelings...and some days it was just better not to ask me to try.

Maybe this will be the year Mel finally gives up on me and refers me to another therapist. What is wrong with me? I have God and one of the best therapists available, and I'm still screwed up and despising life.

I kept feeling my knuckles and wrist bone, trying to soothe myself and not say anything dim-witted. Despite wanting Mel to know everything... I didn't want her to know everything.

Can you go to Heaven if you kill yourself? I guess I'll find out soon...

CHAPTER SEVENTEEN

I sat on the beach, filling my hands with sand and watching the grains slip through my grip. Dusk was fast approaching and it started to rain. I looked out to the ocean; at the waves swirling together in a beautiful symphony. I wondered how much it would hurt to end it all. I didn't want the sweet elderly folk, who strolled the sands at daybreak, to find my body... but perhaps the choppy ocean currents would drift me off to a rocky shore where I wouldn't be found for days... weeks, even. Curling in a ball, I imagined what it would be like to let my lungs fill with water. I was closing in on a strategic plan that I would have to map out with precision. I decided to stop seeing Mel. I didn't want her to recognize how I was declining. I had to be sure the last time I saw her was positive. I also stopped seeing Lindsay, blaming my busyness with work... I guess this wasn't really an issue, considering I hadn't drunk a single drop of alcohol in almost six months.

I was wearing my pretense tighter than ever so there weren't any slip-ups and no-one discovered my plans. I didn't want anyone to stop me. I couldn't let anyone stop me. The only person who probably had some insight into how dark things were turning was Paula. If I cut her out, she would clue into what I was concocting, so I decided to gradually drop off her radar and isolate slowly... so it wasn't obvious. I couldn't let her know how atrocious I was doing. Mentally, physically, spiritually... I was a mess. My insides are rotting away. My bones ached and head hurt. Imaginings of death were igniting like wildfire — taking over every part of my being, smoldering through my hope. I could feel the fissures in my heart exposing the wounds from my childhood...Rejection and shame seeping through.

I just want everything to be better.

The stillness of the night made me so agitated. Sometimes I wanted to run back to my parents' house, nestle in my bed and wake as if none of this had ever happened. I wanted to joke around happily without forcing it all the time. I wanted healthy relationships with guys and to feel secure around men. I wanted a family. I wanted everything I knew wasn't possible.

God, this isn't fair!

Nobody understands how painful everything is. Nobody has all of these messed up parts. Sure, I knew a few people who had one, maybe two; but so many areas of my life were messy. I doubted anyone could look me in the eyes and tell me they completely understood.

Nobody can tell me they understand what it's like to be surrounded by families, yet feel so alone because they can't remember what it's like to be loved... because they can't remember what it's like to belong. Nobody understands how terrifying it is to be totally incapacitated when fearful thoughts dominate their body. Nobody feels so repulsed by their image that they destroy themselves, mentally and physically, in an attempt to ease the hatred. Nobody understands what it is like to lose everything at such a young age.

Sure, some people might relate to some of it... but they cannot understand it all. I just wanted someone to wrap me in a hug and tell me they understood. For someone to let me pour out my fractured heart... with no judgment or sympathy. For someone to tell me I wasn't a horrible person for thinking the thoughts I did and for wanting to die. I just wanted somebody to understand the things I couldn't even explain.

My wrist was once again housing a skin-colored strap. I didn't care what people thought anymore. Covering my wrist was the only thing I could do, unless I didn't want to take proper care of my wounds. People didn't remark on the strapping, however every single person looked at my wrist, then at me, then back to my wrist. I wanted to punch them. Or at least say what they were thinking instead of silently judging me. Despite my permanent wrist accessory, I was still determined to wear a brave disguise. I made plans to go to America to see Jill and Hannah. I was both terrified and excited in the most unusual, indescribable way. People at church were over the moon for me. A few leaders had picked up on how poorly I was doing and they thought going to see Jill and Hannah would help me settle on a healthier track.

Church was the last place I wanted to be. As soon as I stepped inside I was suffocated by anxiety. Honestly, I would rather be drinking or getting high than worshipping in a room full of people. I felt like such an outcast. No matter how I tried to make Sundays easier, I felt so out of place and awkward. Paula insisted that attending church was important. My patience was wearing thin and the only reason I still went every week was because of her.

Keep the act up, Stacey. Keep the act up.

The Senior Pastor invited me to speak at the Easter service and I agreed. I had a dream to be a public speaker and this would be the final time I would ever grace the stage. I knew I had to take care with what I said and make sure people believed my every word. The Easter service was one week before I was booked to leave, and if anyone caught on to what I had planned, it would all be ruined. I wondered if the Senior Pastor would get a word of knowledge[2] from God about what I was devising. Is anyone receiving anything spiritual about me? Is God talking to anyone about what's going on? Maybe God didn't care after all. Could it be, that I was never even saved and that's why hiding my plan has been so easy? Perhaps I won't make it to Heaven. Besides, if somebody had given me a word of knowledge, I would have completely disregarded it. I was flat-face lying to almost every single person; but somehow I thought it would ensure that I didn't hurt them any further.

I sat on the edge of my bed, bound by a formidable fear. I had no idea why I was full of dread, or where it came from. During these random anxiety attacks I would normally lay on the lounge floor; however I could hear my housemate watching a movie, which meant I couldn't. She had no idea how bad I was getting because even the way I acted around the house was a masterfully composed performance. My final months were being precisely planned and executed. Unable to control the thoughts spinning around my head, I had become short of breath. I tried focusing on Jesus... but that didn't work. I tried humming worship songs... but that didn't work. I tried thinking about anything to do with God... but my mind couldn't focus.

---

2 A word of knowledge is the feeling/strong inkling, of knowing what God is doing or about to do in another person's life. Words are to lift people up and breathe life. They are never hurtful, intrusive, or harmful

You are a pathetic, worthless and unlovable fat bitch! Nobody is going to care when you die.

My heart was racing and tears began to traipse down my cheeks. Curled at the end of my bed, I clenched my pillow. I wanted to scream. I wanted to punch the wall. I wanted to fucking die!!! The fear was so tangible that my entire body had shut down. Any desire to live was darkening with each sunset. The only reason I held on was to see Jill and Hannah. I still had to finalize things properly, too... so I couldn't 'check out' just yet. Death consumed my thoughts. If I wasn't obsessing over how I would do it, my thoughts were on what my last posts on social media should be, and whom I should write letters to. I thought about whether to give all my possessions away, or if I should start donating money.

When I wasn't thinking about death, I was bent on destruction. Completely ruining and destroying every inch of my body that I possibly could without accidently dying before the planned date. I reasoned this would make dying that little bit easier. I knew I would have to psych myself up on the day I decided to follow through. I had heard that when you are about to end your life, your mind takes over. Surprisingly, your desire to live heightens and your body fights to survive. I was cutting deeper and more often, making sure I didn't chicken out because of pain. It was a process of desensitizing. On those occasions when cutting wasn't helping, I had also started to burn myself. It was a new technique that was insanely agonizing. The wounds were more difficult to nurse than the cuts and I had to be sure they didn't get infected. Isn't it funny how people who self-harm are experts at wound care! This form of self-love is so twisted. I began purging more and restricting again. I was throwing up more blood than I normally would.

You'll be dead soon, anyway. Get over it.

The only thing I wasn't doing was drinking. I didn't care about sobriety anymore. Sure, it was a God thing that I poured my vodka down the sink after my Baptism. I didn't question that at all. But I no longer want to remain sober because of the stronger Spirit that lived within me. My strategy was that if I didn't drink until the last nights before my plan, the alcohol would mess me up more. My immunity to my red baby would be at an all-time low and I was hoping it would help numb my attempt. I had narrowed my final plan down to two options. I didn't know which I was going to go with, but I definitely had the resources and strength to carry through either plan when the time came.

~

Hundreds of eyes were on me as I walked on the stage.

This is it; this is the last time I will ever do this.

I cleared my throat and grasped the microphone. The dimmed lights obscured most of their faces, except for the first two rows. I wondered if anyone was going to call my bluff or if my elaborate charade would protect my cover. Being on stage meant that hundreds of people would see my wrist all strapped up. My cheeks were puffy and swollen from purging, and my hair was in some serious need of trimming. I looked as good as I felt. I waited for the film behind me to finish. The Senior Pastor wanted me to talk about how my life before becoming a

Christian was similar to the confusion in the clip they had just shown. I felt like a poster girl for abused and broken failures. Whenever people wanted someone to talk about their sad life before Christ, I was pointed out. If a new person came to church and was going through a hardship, people would call on me to go and talk to them. Sometimes I felt like they only saw me for my past... and nobody even really knew the whole story! Everything I was saying was 100% true but to be honest, I didn't believe it anymore. I had no problem lying, but I couldn't handle thinking how all this bullshitting would hurt these precious people once I was gone.

I became emotional as I concluded my speech.

God, don't do this. Don't wreck me now. Not on stage. Please, God.

I didn't try to pretend I wasn't upset. Maybe showing emotion would help my covert operation.

Look everyone! Here are tears! I'm not really void of any feelings right now. I'm not dead already on the inside...

Taking a deep breath, I faced the audience again. Due to my openness about my messed up life, many of them seemed to be in tears themselves. I had no problem discussing my life, however I struggled when people showed me sympathy. Brushing off the emotional moment, I finished strong. I didn't want anyone to question how my relationship with Jesus was at that moment. I didn't want anyone to pray for me. It was my last Sunday at church before going to America and I just wanted people to think I was pumped for my holiday. I didn't want God to break through my walls and save me. I didn't want to have to explain what I was thinking and planning. I couldn't... I would be sent straight back to hospital! As I walked off the stage I received a standing ovation.

If only they knew who they were really clapping.

Someone came up to me after the service and wished me well for my trip to America. Flashing my sham-smile, I hoped they couldn't see through my veneer. I had a lot of respect for the person who stood in front of me. They were such a Godly, humble Child and I didn't want to cause them distress or make them worry.

"Make sure you come home to us, Stace. We're going to miss you..."

How is it that just a few brief words can cause the most heartache? I felt as though I was crumbling.

Make sure you come home...

This church had become my home the second I accepted Jesus into my heart. I felt so supported and welcome here; something I had lacked for the majority of my life. However if this place was home, why would I want to leave so easily? If these people were my family, why was I so hesitant for them to know the truth? Maybe that's the sign of knowing you love someone... when you hide the deepest pain to protect them from being hurt. In reality, I was hurting everyone more by concealing what was really going on. Not that I was hiding things that well. It doesn't take a genius to work out why I was sporting tape around my wrist. Maybe I just didn't know what a home was. Maybe that was the real problem.

"Make sure you come home."

I looked them straight in the eyes and did the one thing I did so well — lied straight through my teeth.

"I will! I'll miss you guys! I'll be back before you know it!"

I felt sick every time I lied, but if I couldn't fool these people, there was no way I would be able to fool Hannah and Jill in a couple of days. I wondered what they would have said if I responded with: "I will! I'll be going home to see our Father very shortly!"

God, will You still welcome me Home? Even if I kill myself?

CHAPTER EIGHTEEN

I made a playlist on my iPod specifically for flying. When I became a Christian I had deleted all my old music. The last time I listened to 'heavy' stuff was the night I threw my Bible across the room after drinking an entire bottle of vodka. I learnt that the music we listen to influences our thoughts and actions; and I had gone to great lengths to ensure everything I was listening to was 'pure' and projecting life and hope. Not anymore! Now, I just wanted to listen to heavy Screamo and depressing break up songs. I no longer cared about the influence music was having in my life.

At the airport I watched everyone stressed out about their connecting flights. People watching is my favorite thing to do, especially when I'm feeling melancholic. I make up stories about people's lives... and wonder if anyone ever watches me, and weaves stories about my life. If they were anything like what I construct about other people, then they were probably spot on with their theories! There were hundreds of people milling around me and ordinarily that would freak me out, but I noticed I wasn't anxious. Normally, I would have been scanning the room for the nearest exit — or infatuated with my phone to avoid eye contact. But here I was... totally fine, sitting calmly, observing the craziness around me. I felt good.

What are you up to, God? I wouldn't be surprised if You did some crazy things on this trip.

Since becoming a Christian, every pre-existing view I had of God had been demolished. He isn't some dude who sits up in the sky, looking down with despairing disappointment... casting judgment when we sin. Rather, He is a living devoted Father, who bestows Love and Healing upon us. His Goodness is renowned for shining the brightest in the darkest times... so that very fact had my defenses ready. I was scared because if God used His power to rescue me, I wouldn't be able to run anymore... I was scared I would have to endure more therapy and medication. I was scared because living wasn't something I want to do... and if He saved me, I might just walk away from Him forever. However, right now I was feeling something unique...

I embraced the anxiety-free moment, as I relaxed back into my seat. I could feel my entire countenance softening, and a calm sensation moving out from my chest to my fingertips. In all my nineteen years, I had never felt so at peace.

God, please let this supernatural peace be with me for the entire trip.

I wandered through the Duty Free shop and paused at the alcoholic section. My red baby was the first thing that caught my eye, and it was less than half the price I would normally spend. Momentarily, my taste buds were tantalized by the smooth texture of vodka. I could feel the sweet burn in my throat. But that was as far as my imagination enjoyed it. I shook my head and rubbed my eyes. The reality was that even after seven months sober, the thought of its flavor made me sick to my stomach. Who would've thought!

I slid up the tiny window shutter and gazed in awe as we flew toward the American shoreline. Over the years I had watched hours of YouTube videos and movies about the USA, but here

I was finally witnessing it with my own eyes! I tried not to look like a lunatic as a ginormous grin danced across my face. I had seen Venice and Santa Monica Beach on my favorite vloggers, and now I was flying over them! I had vicariously lived and breathed everything Californian through the internet... and I couldn't believe I was there!

How surreal.

The plane prepared for landing. I could see concrete buildings stacked all the way to the horizon and highway ribbons stretched out in crisscross formation. Thousands of cars advanced like ants, one after the other, as if in search for the next treasure. I took a deep breath as the plane pulled up on the runway. I had a connecting flight to Texas in four hours, and hoped I didn't freak out whilst trying to find my gate. I had heard so many horror stories about customs... and maybe I had watched one too many custom patrol television shows. What if my luggage was tampered with, or if I told the custom guy I had never actually met the people I would be staying with? I had no idea what you were supposed to do when it came to security checks or passports. I was so out of my comfort zone.

As I waited in line, I remembered a question someone asked me at church:

"Are you scared to travel alone? I mean, travelling to a different country by yourself, especially at a young age. It's a big thing to do!"

I remember the angst I felt when they asked me, and as I looked around at the hundreds of people waiting in line, I finally had an answer to their question. How could I be scared to travel by myself when I had lived almost all my eighteen years alone? Perhaps the peace I was feeling at the airport before leaving Australia was because I was flying away from the horrible history that constantly surrounded me in my home state. Why would I be afraid to travel to a different country when the people here were the only people who loved me for who I was — no matter how broken, upset or stupidly I behaved. Then, just as suddenly as I started to dream about the possibilities of how special this trip would be, depression swept over me - a reminder of my mission at hand.

I was called over to the customs desk, my hands clammy and trembling. The security to enter another country blew my mind. You have to have your eyes and fingerprints scanned, as well as a profile photo.

"What is the purpose of your visit to the United States, ma'am?"

It took every ounce of strength not to reply:

"Oh, just to say goodbye before I die."

"Welcome to Dallas..."

I followed a line of people off the plane and into the airport. My heart was beating fast and my mind preoccupied with so many thoughts about what was going to happen. I didn't want to screw this up. I still wasn't an expert in airports and hoped if I followed the crowd I wouldn't get lost. Accompanied by the clickety-clack of a swarm of cabin bags, we strode up a winding hallway. Fast food stores flanked each side and the wafts of cooking made my stomach growl. I had to figure out how to fly under the radar with my eating. Hannah and Jill both knew I struggled, but they didn't know to what extent. I won't be able to purge at Hannah's, which meant five straight days consuming God-knows-what fatty American food. I drifted from the crowd I was following and went to the bathroom. The airport was small and it seemed my flight was the only one scheduled for the night. Locking myself in a cubicle, I took several deep breaths.

You can do this.
You have to do this.
Breathe!

My eyes started to fill with tears as I thought about how heartbroken Hannah was going to be when she heard I was gone.

I have to make a lot of memories with her so the happy will outweigh the sad. This is the first and very last time I will ever get to see her. What am I supposed to say? Shit.

Scooping up my backpack, I headed out - attempting to find my way to baggage claim in the deserted terminal. I was looking in every direction, trying to spot Hannah. As I took the last turn in the hallway, I saw her. Hannah! Her long dark hair, wearing a T-shirt I sent almost four years ago! I wanted to scream... my body didn't even know how to react! My feet picked up the pace as I closed the remaining space separating us. Her back was turned, so she hadn't sighted me.

Hannah! Hannah! Holy shit... It's Hannah!

My heart was beating uncontrollably. For a moment I forgot about my plan and the depredation I was going to create. In that moment I was just a pen pal who finally, after six years, was meeting her best friend. I could no longer pretend this wasn't the most exciting thing to ever happen... in my entire life! My feet scuffed as I ran awkwardly toward her.

"G'day, mate!"

She looked up and screamed. We had known each other for six years, but never interacted face to face. We had shared so much of our hearts and stories, yet not been present in each other's lives. Somehow, this felt oddly normal. We embraced in one of the longest hugs ever! It felt as though we had grown up together and were being reunited after a semester away at college. Walking down to baggage claim together, we talked nonstop the entire way.

I wished this official introduction were as beautiful as Hannah thought it was. I wished the purpose of my time in America was pure and honest — anything but the reason I ended up coming. I would have to lie to Hannah, Jill and every other person I meet here.

I have to lie and pretend I'm fine. I have to act as though going home isn't returning to hell. I have to whitewash as if I'm going to come back and see them all again soon. I have to lie to the faces of the two people I love the most... and that breaks my damn heart.

Hannah laughed at memes on her phone, totally swept up in emotions. She was so carefree. In the past four days we had gone on so many wild adventures together. It's such an awesome thing to have a friend who lives on the other side of the world... and not just because of the cool gifts they send! More significantly, you form a special bond, a bond that no distance can break. The quiet of night time had been the hardest — when I was alone with my thoughts. I had no idea how I was going to let Hannah know. I was leaving for LA the next day and laboring over what my final words would be. She had no clue of my plans and it absolutely broke my heart. Hannah was the greatest friend I had ever known and the last couple of days with her had reminded me that good people still existed in the world. Yet here I was, convinced I would die next month. The dark cloud above my head was encompassing... and impenetrable. No positive or light thought could overcome the darkness. I felt as though I was being swept up by a tsunami of depression I wasn't strong enough to swim against. I was drowning.

Hannah and I went to the baseball and at the end of the game the lights in the stadium went out as a light show began. Music played and old baseball videos rolled over the big screen. I glanced across to look at Hannah — her face lit up by the hieroglyphic night sky. I thought about how I wanted her to remember me and of us both sitting there in awe of the fireworks, I knew I wanted her to remember me like this. I wanted her to remember the times we were in silent wonderment together. I wanted her to remember the moments our hearts were bouncing with joy as we joked and laughed about ridiculous things. I wanted to make sure there wasn't any time she saw me upset. I didn't want her to know I was overwhelmed with pain. I wanted her to remember my excitement every time we passed a yellow school bus. I wanted her to remember the moments where music washed us with peace. Most of all, I wanted her to remember when we spun on roller coasters — the suspense and thrill that filled our entire beings. I was happy to have had so many awesome days together, but I still felt like I was not leaving her with much to hold on to. For our six years of friendship, I had given her only five 'in real life' days.

I watched as she danced to the music playing from the videos and my heart broke, knowing I was going to cause her so much pain. What are you supposed to say to your best friend in the whole world? What are you supposed to say to anyone for that matter... when you fumble your words and can't form any sense out of the tangled mayhem inside? I wanted to stay in this moment forever. I wanted to be sitting across from Hannah with my heart full of memories, knowing that nothing else mattered. Her heart was too kind, her mind too beautiful, her life too full of goodness to be destroyed by what I was about to do. I wanted to hug her and apologize for everything I was about to put her through.

~

We had planned to go out for breakfast before my flight the next morning, but I woke to Hannah knocking on my bedroom door.

"I have to go to school... I won't be able to come to the airport."

My heart began racing. I now had even less time to work out my final words. I sat in the lounge room as Hannah got ready to leave.

I can't believe this is happening.

I looked around to find a piece of paper and decided I should write a letter to her. At least that way she would be able to keep it and be reminded of everything I want her to know... and also because that's how we became friends — writing letters. I stood at the kitchen island bench, my eyes boring a hole through the blank paper. I started to cry as I thought about all the things I wanted her to know. How could I possibly express my deep love and gratitude for the friendship she gave me? How could I string together the perfect words to thank someone who filled my life with such delight? I hurried to finish the letter as I heard her walking out of her bedroom.

"This sucks so much!"

She piled books in her backpack and stood at the island.

"Dude, I know. I'll be back though."

I started crying as soon as those words plummeted from my mouth. It felt like time began to slow as we looked at each other, our eyes brimming with tears, but our mouths curved into brave grins.

"I'm going to look like a panda bear! Stop making me cry!"

I'm so sorry Hannah. I'm so sorry I'm not strong enough. Sorry I won't be able to come back and do all the things we planned as we grow up. Sorry I'm making you cry now, and for the tears you will cry when you hear about what happens. Sorry I wasn't honest with you. Sorry for hurting you. Hannah... I'm so sorry.

CHAPTER NINETEEN

I cried all the way to the airport. I felt so much guilt knowing my entire time with Hannah wasn't what it should have been. Everything seemed so real now.

One goodbye down. One to go!

I knew it was going to be even harder spending time with Jill and her family. Jill had been amazing during some of my most hectic times. I seriously believe God aligned my path with the internship, so my life could be connected to Jill and richly blessed. She would always text or call anytime I needed to chat... about anything. She was the most non-judgmental person I knew and when I felt like I was a wad of sadness and stupid decisions, sometimes Jill was the only person who just 'got me'. She was the only person I spoke openly and honestly with, so I knew I had to be careful not to let anything slip. Being a mother of two kids close to my age, she had a sixth sense for the unsaid! I felt so disgusting and fat from not purging and eating so much fatty American food... but I knew it was going to be almost impossible to hide any eating behaviors around Jill. She was too smart and never took any bullshit.

God, please give me the strength to be brave. I need to be brave, Lord. I need to be brave...

~

As I gently rocked in the carriage atop the Ferris Wheel, nothing mattered. With views of the entire Santa Monica Beach and Venice in the distance, my mind was able to process everything I had been mulling over since being in America. Spending four days in LA had been a thrill, and a part of me hated that I was keeping up an, 'I-love-my-life' façade. I hadn't bought a single thing, except a Californian key chain from the Santa Monica Pier boardwalk. There was no reason to buy stuff... I was going to be dead in two months.

I gazed out to the ocean, trying to lose myself in the beauty of nature, but I couldn't. I felt numb... so unbelievably numb that if I jumped out of the carriage and plummeted to the boardwalk below, I probably wouldn't feel a thing. Being in the midst of the hustle and bustle of LA is probably daunting for most people, especially if you're a young foreigner... but me? I felt fine! My anxiety, usually a daily struggle, was non-existent there. Maybe God was allowing me to enjoy this time so I knew what a holiday was before I died? The only thing I was excited about was hiking the Runyon Canyon and walking from Santa Monica to Venice. There was no way I was going to die before seeing all those sights they had to offer.

I closed my eyes as the Ferris Wheel continued to rotate. Being the only one in the carriage, I just wanted to linger — for hours — soaking it all in. I had seen these views countless times on Youtube and in movies... now I was finally here. Even if for the wrong reasons, I was here! I had no idea what I would say to Jill when I left. LA had given me the space to think; but is there ever enough time to conclude what you will say to someone you love for the very last time? Everything I considered didn't capture how significant she was to me or how thankful I was for her... How grateful I was to have spent time with her and her family. I'm glad I'm going to die knowing what it's like to feel wanted and a part of a family.

My carriage reached the bottom and the lady controlling the Ferris Wheel spun her finger around in a circle, indicating there was one more round before it stopped.

Please just let me stay on. Just a little longer... please...

I looked out towards Venice and saw people, like tiny insects, covering the boardwalk. Everything seemed tranquil up high. Closing my eyes, I listened to the carnival games below and wondered what it would be like if I hadn't visited as a final goodbye. I wondered what life would be like if I could go on holidays for all they were intended — to recharge and make memories. I wondered what it would be like if my life was entirely different. I reached for my bag and waited for the carriage to stop swaying. My feet settled on the wooden boardwalk and I headed for Venice. All these things were pointless... nothing seemed worthwhile knowing I was just going to die soon. But it felt good, if only for a moment, that nothing else mattered. Temporarily, I was caught in the busyness of Venice and all LA life had to offer... forgetting what awaited me back home. I was able to briefly disregard that fact that I was sad and wanted to die. Maybe God is telling me there are better things ahead and I need to hold on? Or maybe I'm thinking way too much about everything and just need to be brave, finish this trip and do all I came here to do — say goodbye.

I sat across from Jill on the couch, a nightly ritual that had filled me with immense pleasure over the last couple of days. I would miss these moments where we chatted about our day and commentated whatever show was on the TV. The peace I felt at the airport returned again the moment I touched down in LA. Every day in California was filled with such a buffering sense of rest, my heart had been at ease. Every street was unknown but I felt as though I had walked it a thousand times. Each store was a fresh experience, but it was like I had been grocery shopping there for years. Then there were moments every day when I was jolted from my trance and reminded of why I was there. I spent most of my days journaling, drawing or watching TV. It was hard being around such a close family unit. Difficult, because my heart was so happy, although knowing I could never have what they had. I watched as they went about their daily routines and how they co-existed with one another. I watched as they re-solved arguments and misunderstandings in a non-violent, non-threatening manner. They demonstrated what a real family was like — and I wished I wasn't going to die. I wished I could have what they had. I wished I was filled with hope, enabling me to look forward to the future and possibilities that might await me. I wished I could confidently say I was excited to be a mother and have a husband cheering me on through every season... and children who I raised to be contributing members of society. I wanted that so intensely. However my compulsion to die and leave all the pain behind me was even stronger than my desire to start fresh and create my own family.

"I'm so glad I came when I did."

"Well, I'm glad you're here!"

Shut the fuck up, Stacey! You've come this far already... don't blow it now!

I hadn't spent any solid time with God since being in America and I hadn't felt this distant from Him since before becoming a Christian. I would always take time to purposely pray or spend time with Him. I would be so hungry to discover His heart, get lost in the Bible and dream with Him. The only time I had intentionally spent with God was when I asked Him to help with my plan. Even though He felt so distant, I knew the Holy Spirit was doing something within me and I wasn't resilient enough to fight and win.

"I'm in a really bad place, Jill. I had to come now."

Shut.
The.
Fuck.
Up!!!!!!

Jill looked at me, confused. Putting down her iPad, she sipped her wine (Classic Jill!), and leaned over to me. My whole body was tingling and my mind was racing. I had no idea what I was going to say, but I knew it didn't matter because the Holy Spirit was stirring me to blurt out the truth — whether I liked it or not. I started to choke up and rubbed my eyes trying to push back at the tears that were starting to fall.

"It's okay baby girl... you can cry. What's going on?"

I was fighting so hard, not only to hold back tears; but to stop myself from telling her what was really happening. I didn't want to share anything. I just wanted to pretend I was having a bad day and being over-emotional. I didn't want her to know. I *couldn't* let her know. She would be shattered! While I was processing internally, I knew the Holy Spirit had taken over and my mouth had spilled the beans! I'm not sure to what extent, but she knew. I watched as she turned from bewilderment to brokenness. Sadness seeped into her eyes and her face drooped.

GOD, WHAT ARE YOU DOING?!
STOP!!!!!

"You can't do this! You can't! Do you know how upset I would be? Stacey... you can't!"

But I need to. Jill, I fucking need to!! I can't keep on living like this.

I slumped further into the couch, wishing I never sat down and opened myself up to this conversation. I hated God for taking control. I hated that He wanted the best for me and didn't want me dead. I hated that He knew I wouldn't listen to Him, so He was sharing my intentions with the people I loved the most.

"You can't do this. You can't do this."

She kept repeating herself over and over again. But I felt numb. I felt so incredibly detached, I had no idea what to think or do. I wasn't even a tiny bit guilty seeing how distressed she was getting. She moved over to the corner of the couch where I was sitting and embraced me.

"I love you too much. Please don't. You can't do this, Stacey."

My body became limp as I bundled up in her arms. I couldn't cry or show any emotion. Nor could I close my eyes to block out what was happening. I stared straight ahead, smelling her perfume as she embraced me. The closer she pulled me in... the more my emotions reignited. I had never been held like this. I have never had someone show me such compassion and acceptance through an embrace. I started to become undone, because I understood this was what it felt like to have a mother. Of course this was normal for a mother to do with her child... yet I was shocked someone actually wanted to be so close to me. I was shocked that someone who wasn't biologically related to me, wanted to embrace me in that way. That someone knew my darkest secrets and yet still loved me.

I'm so sorry, Jill.

Jill was still holding me and I listened as she began to sob. I didn't want this to happen... to put a downer on the fun we'd been having. I didn't want to leave on a bad note. I had worked so hard to make sure my final moments were filled with joy and positivity and now I had gone and blown it.

I've fucking blown it!!!

"You can't go home. Please just stay here a little longer."

I knew she was going to try all she could to convince me not to follow through with my plan. I knew she was going to watch me extra close and pick up even the slightest negativity in me.

I've gone this far and worked so hard to prepare, I'm not backing out now.

"I can only stay for maybe a week longer. But that's it."

My visa permitted me to remain in America 90 days which meant technically I could stay much longer. I didn't care about anything back home. Not the people, the church, my job, my future there... nothing. I didn't have a family or anyone waiting for me. I could stay the whole ninety days to make Jill happy, but I knew I shouldn't. I couldn't keep changing my plans and the date I was going to die. I'd made a commitment and I had to stick to it.

"Promise me you won't. You can't. Baby girl... please... I love you too much."

I clenched my teeth, knowing I was about to break the biggest rule I had for myself – never lie to Jill.

"I promise."

CHAPTER TWENTY

I couldn't erase the image of Jill from my mind. The way she enveloped me — and rocked me back and forth — trying to calm me down and change my mind... it destroyed me! I felt even more pathetic and guilty than I had before. I didn't want to see anyone's reactions, let alone Jill's. I didn't want to see a preview of the devastation I was about to create. Was that selfish? Probably. But I didn't care anymore. I didn't understand how someone could go through so many horrible circumstances and still want to live. In the span of a year, I had been homeless, admitted to a psych ward, more depressed than ever before, and contemplated my own death far more than enjoying the beauty of life. I was two months from turning nineteen and all I had achieved was to be subjected to evil masterminds who caused me to hate every inch of myself. I had no idea what love was, especially in the context of a family — a *real* family — who accepted and loved me unconditionally. I still couldn't understand why God let everything happen this way. Where was He when my innocence was being taken at such a young age? Why didn't He protect me from all the monsters? Why did He allow so much heartache and devastation to plough through my life?

Why didn't you help me, God?

Jill wasn't going to be back by the time I left for Australia... I was so relieved. We hadn't said a proper goodbye, because she thought she would be back in time from her business trip. I was disappointed that one of her last memories of me was when I told her I wanted to die, however, I was relieved I wouldn't have to hold it together on the day of my departure. It was going to be tasking enough saying goodbye to her husband and daughter. At least I had a private town car driving me to the airport. That way, I could cry as much as I wanted and not worry about the driver.

I sat on the edge of my bed, trying to muster up the motivation to start packing my suitcase. As much as I was ready to leave and pull together the finishing touches to my plan, I wasn't exactly ready. I was scared. I was petrified of failing and breaking the hearts of the people I loved so dearly. I knew if I failed, I would have to see Jill completely heartbroken. Worse than how she was the other night. I would have to see Hannah filled with grief and there would be so many questions to answer. I also knew that if I was successful, like I hoped... they would be left without answers — with heavy burdens and a ghastly pain I could have stopped. I imagined how they would remember me. Worse still, I imagined how they would find out. I didn't want them to hear I was dead from social media... but I couldn't run the risk of sending them a text and having them intervene. Physically, their distance would work to my advantage; but emotionally, it would cause the most heartache. Those in my home state would be able to mourn together. If someone ended up throwing a celebration or funeral, they would at least have one another. It grated on my heart that neither Hannah nor Jill would have that. And that was the hardest thing to accept.

I'm so sorry.

~

Reality hit me as the plane touched down on my home soil. I was rocked with the sudden realization that this was actually happening. I had completed my final mission: to make sure Hannah and Jill had some memories to hold on to. I had experienced everything I had been dreaming about for years and see the only two people who I honestly cared about.

Now, it was done.

It seemed like I had only just arrived in LA and here I was, back where I started. Even though I would have liked to spend more time in America, I was on a tight schedule and needed to execute my plan perfectly. I refused to allow myself to fall in love with life, even if it was genuine. I couldn't get excited only to fall back down in six months and want to die again. I was in a never-ending cycle of false highs and bottomless lows... and it was time to end it all. Now it was time for the hard stuff!

I had calculated just one month 'til D-day. I wasn't as worried about making sure those in my hometown remembered me positively. Everybody already knew I was messed up. Sure, a few people would remember me for my humor and quick wit but many would recall me as a sour, sad bitch. I was fine with that. It was going to take too much time and energy to ensure everyone had a good memory with me. I had to focus on my plan and settle everything before the end. I returned to an empty home. My housemate was away for a few days, which meant I could catch up on all the damaging behaviors I hadn't partaken in while Stateside! Dumping my suitcase in my room, I headed straight to my bedside table where my silver weapon was concealed. Holding the blade between my fingers, I drew in deep. Like an addict, I was craving this feeling and felt relieved as soon as the blade made contact with my skin.

My stomach was furrowed with pink fleshy scars that I wasn't game enough to cut over. Although my wrist was my usual canvas of choice, there was still room. I was an idiot for choosing to cut there — as it is the most obvious area everyone checks when they know you self-harm. Walking to the bathroom, I sat on the floor in front of the toilet, taped my freshly lined wrist and looked toward the bowl. In the last twenty four hours, I had eaten a bagel and two coffees, so I definitely had something to get out. Clamping the edge of the toilet bowel with one hand, I forced my fingers down my throat with the other.

Get it all out, you fat bitch! You have three weeks to make up for!!

My head became faint and I fell back. My stomach was sore and one of my knuckles had started to bleed from hitting my front teeth. I was coughing but didn't care. There was nobody who would hear and become concerned. I wish I lived by myself again — at least then I could do whatever I wanted without the apprehension of someone hearing or walking in on me. I jabbed my fingers back down my throat and continued to make up for the mistakes I had eaten in America. My throat soon became dry and sore and my jaw ached.

Displeased with my attempts, I went back to my room for a cigarette. I was fully committed to destroying my body in every way possible, even if that meant smoking and doing drugs again. Sitting on the back step, I lit up. The lady next door could see me from her window but I didn't care. Why should I?

I watched the afternoon sky slowly defer to the night. The blue transitioned to soft shades of pink, and the birds returned to the treetops to nest. I started crying as I inhaled longer drags of nicotine. My hand was a bloody mess from my knuckles and my wrist had started to sting. I was numb from the cold air and the reality of what was unfolding. The more I thought about what I needed to do, the more I cried. Flicking my cigarette onto the grass, I went back inside to get another one. Suddenly there was a knock on the door. Sheathing my wrists with my sleeves, I opened the door.

It was the lady from next door.

"Hi sweetie. I was just about to duck outside but you came in before I had the chance. Are you okay?"

God, there is no way You're using this lady to get to me. Stop!

"Oh, yeah! I'm fine!"

I offered a smile, but I'm sure it translated as a grimace. My eyes were bloodshot from crying and purging and my nose was running from sitting out in the cold.

Why are old people so nosey?

"I saw you were upset. Are you sure you're okay sweetie?"

Lay off with the fucking sweeties!!

"Yeah, I'm sure!"

I took a step back and reached for the door handle, hoping she would take the damn hint that I didn't want to talk to her.

"Okay. Well if you ever need someone to talk to or even just listen to whatever is going on, you can always pop around! I can make us a cup of tea!"

In all the months I have lived here, I have never had a conversation with this woman. The most interaction we had was when I hung washing on the line and she walked by to say hello... to which I only ever replied with a smile.

No talking. No fucking cups of tea and free therapy sessions. Nothing.

"Thanks."

I slammed the door, knowing I probably broke her old heart... *but seriously, fuck her!*

I grabbed a jacket and two more cigarettes and walked across the road to the beach. I hadn't been able to get behind the wheel of a car without having a major panic attack, which not only frustrated me; but made me feel like such a failure. Everyone else my age has their licence and are driving around without a care in the world... and I can't even get behind the damn wheel without emotionally breaking down! I was so blessed to live close to the beach. I think if I lived anywhere else I would definitely have killed myself by now. The beach was my 'safe place'... where I could simply relax and forget about things for a while. Like most days, it was deserted. I sat close to the water's edge and watched the wave's crash in closer toward me.

God, I'm not going to listen to anyone... no matter who it is you send to save me. I won't listen, to them — or to You. Just stop!

I hadn't even been home twelve hours and already was aware that "home" wasn't actually home. The beach was the only place that felt right but everything else... far out!! I feel so displaced. I was more at home in California than here. Even though I had walked nearly every street here more than a hundred times, I felt like I was more comfortable with the hustle and bustle of LA. I hugged my knees into my chest, shielding myself from the chilly sea breeze. I was absolutely miserable.

I HATE this town.

I punched the sand as I cried... again. I can't be this emotional around people... my cover will be blown. I couldn't afford to see anyone — so it would be easier to stick to what I had planned. I was panicked I would disintegrate and miss my goal. I was worried I would take heed to all the bullshit people fed me, and believe I was buoyant enough to charter the right course again. Isolating myself would be too obvious, but if I went into avoidance mode and wore my mask... I doubted anyone would pick up on the deception. The only person I had to fool was Paula and I knew that was going to be a tremendous act to pull off.

CHAPTER TWENTY ONE

My original planned date had to change because there was no doubt that Jill would be on my back, constantly checking in with me. I didn't want to be alive for my nineteenth birthday but I knew in order to fool everyone, I had to bite the bullet. Pushing the date back meant I had more time to plan everything. It also meant I was guaranteed to have the house to myself...

God Bless my housemate and her social life!

I set the new date for a week after my birthday. I couldn't hold on any longer. Every day I woke and didn't die, the darkness dragged me deeper into its lair of hopelessness. Someone might notice I was gone before my housemate returned, so I decided my bed would be the place where they (whoever 'they' ended up being) would discover me. I wanted to avoid involving people as much as possible. This ruled out leaping in front of a vehicle, public hanging, jumping off a bridge or drowning in the ocean. I don't want to be a bloody mess either, which ruled out cutting. The only thing left that was sure to work was suffocation.

I knew you could die if you bound a bag over your head for long enough, but I needed to make sure it was possible to succeed with suicide by this method. I Googled every possible thing about suffocation as a form of suicide and then committed to doing it. If I failed, the chances of brain damage were highly likely. No matter what method I chose, I knew it would be risky and incredibly frightening if I survived. However, my intention to die was stronger than caring about living with impaired brain function.

~

"What's all this?"

Paula strode through the door with a shopping bag and pillow tucked under her arm. We had arranged a coaching session, weekly as normal, however I had no idea why she had all the props.

"It's for you!"

She walked past toward the lounge where she revealed what was inside the bag — a new bed set! Quilt, sheets... everything!

"God told me to buy you a brand new bed spread."

I was speechless. Accepting gifts is something I was woeful at, but I was more gob smacked by the fact God was trying to break down my walls — with sweet gestures like this! I couldn't quite understand the reason why He spoke to Paula about doing this, or what the deep meaning was, however I thought it was comical!

A new bed spread to die in? Okay, God.

Paula suggested that seeing a therapist again would be a good idea; but I didn't want to. A Christian therapist would probably help me understand some of the deeply rooted issues that kept messing me up... but I couldn't do it. If I wasn't able to see Mel, I didn't want to go to anyone. If I saw someone in the next three weeks... before I planned to die... I would get sent to hospital again. They would psycho-analyze what was going on in my head. I could fool anyone, except probably not a qualified therapist.

"I'm fine. I might get in contact after my birthday sometime. I'm doing good right now."

It was likely Paula didn't believe a single word-bubble from my pretend character; but I couldn't throw up the white flag and let her convince me to talk to someone. I had seen a therapist before my trip to America and I hated it. I was expected to talk about issues I had never told anyone before. It provoked regular flashbacks, and my sleep was overtaken by nightmares, paralyzing me with fear. I couldn't spend another minute entertaining a stranger with the story of my rampageous life. I couldn't bear more notes to be taken about me... nor could I stomach unearthing everything I had buried for years. I didn't see how talking about abuse could possibly help ease the pain that years of trauma had caused. How could talking to someone take the flashbacks and nightmares away? How could it help allay my crushed spirit? Sharing my anguish with a therapist would only make everything worse. Besides, I was so awkward I would never know how to communicate what was reeling around my head. Mel had known me long enough to understand when I couldn't handle deep questions... She also knew when to incite me to dig a little deeper.

Why can't I just walk into a therapist's office and say:
"Hi. My name is Stacey and I was abused since I was a child. Now I hate every inch of my body... which has become a breeding ground for my eating disorder and depression. I drink every day just to give me enough courage to face what

lies ahead, and I'm afraid every person I meet is going to hurt me. Instead, I hurt myself — with a special blade. I have severe anxiety attacks. I thought sleeping with someone I loved would help me feel better... but it made things worse. Everywhere I turn, I'm reminded of people who laid hands on me... and I just want to die. I'm done."

Could I just waltz in, spout my spiel, and be healed?

Even if that did happen, I think I would still want to die. There's only a certain amount a person can go through until life becomes unbearable... no matter how "healed" or strong I may be. There's a certain level of darkness that I felt I couldn't be saved from. I knew if I talked long enough Paula would be able to break my walls down and the Holy Spirit would be quick to fill my mind with the truths of God. I didn't want that. The Holy Spirit is gentle and doesn't force, which is exactly the same for God... but I knew He was going to pull all sorts of tricks while Paula was still there. If I allowed the Holy Spirit to have His way, even in just a small part of me, I would be lost to His wooing.

This would be the last time I saw Paula. This would be the last time I saw anyone before I died. I knew God was prompting her, to have her do and say all sorts of things in an attempt to save me. So, I put my walls up... and shut down. It was dumb to be quiet, but I would rather take my chances than open up to the risk of encountering God in a way I had been avoiding for months. However, the thing about Paula is that even when I didn't say a single word, even if I sat in complete silence... the presence of God was always so strong. She carries Jesus in a way that is unique and incredibly powerful. I sat next to her, biting my lip and trying not to be transparent. I knew she was praying in her head — pleading with God to break through to me.

"So what else has been going on?"

Oh, not much. Just planning my suicide for this weekend.

"Nothing, really. Just the usual... chilling."

I don't know how Paula puts up with me sometimes. Between my sarcastic comments and avoiding every problem, I would have walked out on me long ago. What freaked me out when I first became a Christian, had become an everyday occurrence. When the Presence of God (like a weighty peace) became strong, things like manifestations (which can look like a Tourette's tic) and speaking in tongues / Heavenly Language, were as normal to me as any other daily task. I'm incredibly sensitive to the workings of the Holy Spirit, so, when I'm in a positive headspace and close in my relationship with God, I can pick up almost immediately when there's something dark happening in the room.

Weird tingling sensations shot across my body as soon as I replied to Paula. I tried shifting on the couch, to defer the feelings from consuming me. Despite wanting to die so badly, I knew there was a small part of me holding on. That part would ruin my plan, so I had to make sure I did all I could to ignore it and forget it was there. I tried to act normal as The Holy Spirit was pressing to break through.

Paula, stop praying!!!!

I fumbled my way through pointless conversation until Paula realised she wasn't going to get anything out of me. It was obvious she knew something was up. I followed her to the door.

"I'll pick you up for church on Sunday?"

This was it... time to say goodbye to someone who had invested so much into me. Time to shoot an arrow straight through her heart.

"Umm, I might not be at church this week. I have plans."

I smiled, trying to hide the unvarnished truth bubbling over inside me. I stood in the doorway, fidgeting with the door handle... a sign I was nervous. Paula eyed me with the same tender look she gave when she knew I was self-harming again. The same look she gave every time she knew something was wrong.

"Stacey..."

She took a step closer to the door, as if she wanted to come back inside. I couldn't let her stay longer. I turned the light on outside hoping to indicate it was perfectly fine to stay outside and chat.

"It's all gee. Seriously!"

"All gee? That's a new one. Seriously Stacey, what is going on?"

Her voice became firm as I stood in the doorway, blocking her from attempting to come back inside.

"Nothing! I've just got things planned. It's good though... seriously."

I shifted my feet back and forth.

I hate lying! I'm so pathetic... lying straight to her face.

Her brow furrowed and she looked at me with a sense of despair that was heart breaking.

"Come stay at my house for the weekend."

God, stop talking to her!!

Paula knew I didn't cope with being alone, especially when I wasn't doing well. She knew everything I got up to when I was left alone with my own thoughts. She knew something was up... but I couldn't let her in on it.

It's a kind gesture, but I can't accept. This has all worked out perfectly; I won't get another chance to be home alone for so long — at least several more months. I have to die this weekend. It can't be postponed again.

"Aww, thanks. It's okay, though. I have some stuff to do here."

"Are you sure?"

Gut-wrenching sorrow filled both Paula and I. I'm not sure if she could see the sadness that swept over me, but I could definitely feel it. I wasn't sure if Paula looked concerned because I refused to go stay with her, or because she knew something bad was going to happen. It was obvious God was communicating with her, otherwise she wouldn't be trying so hard to knock my walls down and get me out of the house. She opened her arms and pulled me into a warm hug, probably another attempt to get me to speak... or cave in and accept her offer.

"Love you..."

Oh man. Oh man. Fuck. I'm so sorry, Paula. I'm so so sorry!

"I love you, too."

I tried not to cry as we held eye contact until the darkness of the night concealed our faces.

I'm so sorry, Paula.

CHAPTER TWENTY TWO

I grasped the pen so tightly my hand began to turn red.

I wasn't strong enough to keep fighting.
Sometimes really horrible things happen, making it really hard to breathe again.
I couldn't escape the bad stuff.
I had nothing left to give.
To my blood family — I left way before you saw me for the last time.
Don't cry over a life you created and then helped destroy.
To my non-blood family — I love you all and I'm sorry. Thank you for you... for the laughs and the adventures. Thank you for everything. Remember all the good times. Have a dance party for me... and turn the music up loud!
I love you guys. I really am sorry.
Do great things with your life. Never give up on your dreams.
Do you. You've got this! Xo

I didn't know what else to say or if what I wrote was deemed worthy enough to cover the pain this was going to cause. I couldn't say sorry enough, and even though I knew apologizing wasn't going to make anything better... that is all I wanted to say. My mind was foggy from my jumbled thoughts and the alcohol I had consumed since lunch. I read the letter over and over again, each time crying a little more than the last.

This is it. This is really it.

I placed it on my bedside table so it wouldn't go unseen. Perched on the end of my bed, I drew in deep, long breaths, trying to psych myself up for what I was about to do. My bedroom felt ten times bigger, making me seem tiny in comparison. Despite my heart beating out of control, the stillness of everything around me was spooky. I couldn't hear any outside noise - not the ocean or passing cars. Nothing. It was as if nature was holding its breath... awaiting my next move. Grabbing my phone, I opened the Instagram app. I had posted a photo of Hannah and I with a note that she would be oblivious to. I took a screen shot of a list of songs I wanted people to play if they held a remembrance service for me, and captioned it with "Pour one out for me."

Come All You Weary by Thrice

Hello, I'm in Delaware by City and Color

Your Hand in Mine by Explosions In The Sky

It's Not Enough by Dustin Kensrue

I clutched the bag to my heart as I lay there.

If I fail this, I could be a potato for the rest of my life. And if it doesn't fail that badly, I will be a potato regardless because of the numerous anti-depressants forced down my throat. I have three days without anyone thinking something is wrong. Sunday is questionable... people (especially Paula) may start to worry, but I definitely have a solid twenty four hours to get this done! The alcohol was making this process less scary than it would have been sober. I took a deep breath and placed the bag over my head, making sure I blocked any entrance for oxygen. The bag crinkled with every breath — a haunting presence. I wished I had worked out a way to listen to music to distract myself. My concept of time ceased to exist. My breathing was shallow, and my head throbbing with pain. My body became limp... and my hands — scrunched tightly into fists — fell open.

~

You're such a failure! You even failed at killing yourself! Stupid fucking bitch!!

I woke up not knowing if I was dead, or in some hypnagogic transition between Heaven and hell. It took me several minutes before I saw the bag next to me.

I failed. I fucking failed! Didn't I do everything right! How did the bag get off my head?!?!

I rolled out of bed and moved sluggishly toward the bathroom. I couldn't recognize the person staring back at me. Her eyes were red and lifeless and her skin had turned a sallow grey.

Stupid! Stupid, stupid, fucking stupid!!!!

I fell to the floor, bawling. The reality of failing was exasperating; I didn't want to accept defeat. If this was God's way of saving me, it wasn't going to work. I had planned this for such a long time. I had postponed it once, and now gone so far... failing was not going to stop me. I had a backup plan: hanging. However, I didn't have the strength to do that... at least not just yet. My breathing slowed and my mind felt peaceful as I reached for my backup bag. I didn't feel guilty or scared. I already knew what it was like. I was ready, probably more than last night. I lay back in bed and stared at the ceiling. This time, I could hear everything... the birds chirping and the breeze blowing in the distance. I closed my eyes and held the bag over my head, making sure there was no way it could come off.

Just let me die, God. Fucking let me die, dammit!!

I began taking slow, deep breaths... hoping I would pass out quicker. The sound of the bag crackling with every breath was still as chilling as last night.

Let me go, God! Let me go!!

My head started to get hazy and I was breathing deeper. My eyes rolled back and I started to lose consciousness. Everything went black, but my heart was still beating.

I need to die. Let me fucking die, God!

My eyelids flew opened as I started to panic. The lack of alcohol in my system was making this a lot harder than before. I couldn't remember this phase. I didn't remember it being this scary. My breathing became faster, my heart began to beat uncontrollably, and my ears were ringing. The air in the bag was running out. My heart felt as though it would jump out of my chest at any moment. Despite the pitch black and the bag over my head, I could see my surroundings clearly. Thick webbing covered the entire ceiling, except it didn't look like the elegant, silky webs spiders weave. They appeared heavy and spooky, like Halloween decorations.

Was I in hell?

It was far from the 'weeping and gnashing of teeth' the Bible talks about. But it *felt* like hell... gruesome and terrifying. All of sudden, amidst the darkness and despair, I felt God's presence. Although the room was dark and the bag over my head muted my vision, I could feel Him right next to me. Right beside my bed! I hadn't felt His presence like this for months. Why was He doing this now?

God, I don't want you! I want to fucking die! Let me die!!

I became immobilized. Not because of fear, or lack of oxygen to my brain. I became paralyzed with His Love! I could not move a single muscle! It felt as though God was chuckling... as if this wasn't scary or too problematic for Him to conquer. I started to cry. Not because I knew my walls had finally been broken, but because His presence was so real. I continued lying there, weeping and being embraced with His precious Love. At some point, the bag had come off and was now on the other side of the room. I was still completely unable to move. My breathing finally calmed down and my heart steadied to a normal pace. The cobwebs, like the bag, had vanished.

I had failed. I had failed for a second time.

But I wasn't disappointed or angry with God. Instead, my heart was full of thankfulness. I couldn't feel the dysphoria that had plagued my heart for years. My mind, although it had just been deprived of oxygen, felt so clear and at peace. I didn't even feel faint as I eventually got out of bed. Instead, I felt strong. Even though I could no longer sense God's presence, I knew He was still fighting for me. I understood I was in a battle much greater than I could fathom. The depth I had sunk to, whether I chose it or not, had blinded me from the truth He was showing me. I walked to the lounge room and fell on to the couch, weeping again.

I sent a text to four close friends, including Paula and Georgina. I didn't want to tell them what had just happened, but knew I needed to have people praying for me. After the messages sent, I threw my phone on the other side of the couch.

What are you supposed to do when you fail a suicide attempt? How are you supposed to look your loved ones in the eye and tell them how close you were to not being here anymore?

Up to this point, my entire life had been hard... but I had gone and made things a whole different kind of hard. I hadn't planned a single thing past this point, because I wasn't supposed to be alive anymore. I had no idea what I was supposed to do.

God, what am I supposed to do?

CHAPTER TWENTY THREE

Hardly anyone knew what happened a month earlier. It was like some ghoulish secret entombed at my core. I walked around with a smile, acting as if I nothing happened. I was thankful God saved me. I really truly was, but a part of me still didn't know how to handle everything. Each day I woke to the knowledge of how I should have been dead... how blessed I should feel at getting another chance...

But I didn't.

I feel lost.

Drastically lost.

On the opening day of our church's annual conference, I sat close to the stage, cloaked in bravado. I hadn't thought I would be alive to register, and honestly, I wasn't even sure if I wanted to be there. I hadn't attended or helped at the weekly youth group because my anxiety was always shooting through the roof. I wasn't robust enough to mingle among crowds of people, their conversations, their inquiries. The leaders probably thought I was unreliable because I was always pulling out of commitments. I couldn't stop wondering why God saved me a month ago. I had hoped things were going to dramatically change, but not a single damn thing had improved! If anything, it had just become worse. I was still struggling with my eating and self-harming. Sure, I didn't want to die anymore, but I still felt like shit. The only thing that changed was my relationship with God. I guess that's something... and something incredible, at that! I felt His presence more frequently. I was definitely seeking Him more than in those months leading up to my suicide attempt.

God, please do something radical during this conference. Please show me that You have a reason for saving me.

I closed my eyes and listened to the guest speaker. Everything he was preaching stirred my spirit. I began to feel like I did when I first became a Christian, when I had that touch from Heaven. I moved to the front as worship began. My entire body was tingling and I knew the Holy Spirit was preparing me for an awesome encounter. I hadn't opened my heart to Him in a raw, transparent way for so many months.

As soon as I closed my eyes and raised my hands, every single wall collapsed. All my doubts and fears about Him and why He saved me dissipated. The youth pastor jumped on stage and began to declare and speak life into the lives of people in the building. He was preaching the first time I came to church and I will forever remember what he talked about. He remains one of my favorite pastors and I value every prophetic declaration he delivers. Some people know about God, but he *knows* God... knows him in such an intimate way that is evident when you have a conversation with him.

I bit my lip as he continued to decree and prophesy.

"If you feel like there are some things causing you fear or anxiety that you are wrestling to let go... if you need the help of our Creator, to remove it... to take the pressure off... to take the weight off. I believe you're going to feel lighter. I believe you're going to sense it physically. You're going to feel different. There's going to be a shift in your heart."

My chest tightened with anxiety. I tried to focus on my breathing to settle myself down. I was listing everything that caused me anxiety and pleading with God to take it all away.

"I believe there is someone here who is feeling uncomfortable in their chest because of fear. I want you to put your hand on your chest right now."

My hand was shaking tremulously as I raised it to my chest. The youth pastor began to pray, declaring peace and freedom... for a sound mind and for depression and anxiety to go in Jesus' name.

Breathe, Stacey. Breathe! Just breathe!

"I believe there are also people in this room who, when you think about someone, you shake from fear. God wants to set you free."

I started crying. Everything he was saying was spot on. Every distress and trepidation I had listed... All I had been suffering.

Thank You, God!

After praying, he asked everyone who put their hand on their chest, to clench their hands into a fist and then open it back up. This physically represented letting go - of the anxiety, the fear, the worries. With my hand still trembling, I clenched my hand into a fist... then opened and closed it for everything I listed. I started speaking in tongues as my hand opened and closed into a fist.

Is this what you saved me for, God? Is this your radical sign?

The guest speaker came forward and announced he had words for people. I always got excited when someone on stage pointed out a person in the crowd to prophesy over them. I would sit up tall, hoping and praying it would be me. But right now, I didn't want to hear what God might be saying about me. I tried to become inconspicuous, hoping the guest speaker would highlight another person.

"Girl with the purple, blue hair. Come here. I like you, you're cool!"

God, no! Not today!

I look around, hoping somebody else had the same hair color as me! Unfortunately not!

Ambling forward, I hoped by the time I reached the front God would have decided not to continue. Awkwardly, I stood at the platform with hundreds of people staring at me. Thankfully one of my good friends followed and stood right next to me, rubbing my back to comfort and reassure me it was going to be okay. I don't know what I would have done without her.

"God showed me a picture of a canvas. He said it's time to paint with more color. There are colors you've put away because of other's expectations."

I looked at my friend who was grinning in disbelief.

This is so insane!! Hardly anyone knows about my artwork or that I've stopped doing any form of art. This is crazy!

"I see that when people look at your art, they get healed. You've seen things that no one else will understand. And you've put your pallet away, saying, 'They won't get it.' That's the point!"

Breathe, Stacey. Breathe... just breathe!

I didn't want to cry in front of so many people, but everything he was saying was accurate. It struck me straight in the heart! I looked across to my friend again, who was almost in tears at how remarkable this was.

"God is saying 'I talk to You in a unique way! Don't be, or conform to, any other standard except the unique, divine design that's in you.' It's going to get messy, scary, wonderful. Messy! But it's all God!"

I took a deep breath and glanced to my side to see if my friend was still there. Everything was becoming such a blur and I didn't want her to leave my side. Everything that was being spoken over me was exciting... but also incredibly terrifying.

"What you do visually, changes people physically! This is your space to be the authentic you that you're called to be. It's time to bring back the creativity!"

Wow, God. Wow!

~

The next morning, I woke feeling refreshed. I had made it through an entire day without having one anxiety attack! I put some worship music on and begin to prepare my heart for the night session. I had never taken my eating disorder to God, because I didn't consider it to be a problem. Technically, I wasn't thin enough to be officially diagnosed with anorexia. But while I was soaking in the Heavenly lyrics, my heart began to pour out all my fears regarding food. The one thing I thought I would never address was now flowing out as if it were the only thing I wanted to talk about. God's presence became so strong it reminded me of how I felt a month ago. He was so real and tangible, I began crying.

My precious daughter, you are made in My image.
You are worthy and beautiful.
You walk with grace and strength.
You are strong and mighty.
You are brave and smart.
My child, I love you.
I love you at your worst and at your best.
My love for you is infinite.
Nothing can change that.
Let Me fix your eyes to see what I see.
Let Me.
Let me, my precious one.
You are beautiful.
I love you.

I had asked God to do something radical and show me that saving me was for something... that being alive was worth it. What if the radical sign was more insane than I could ever imagine? I spent more time being still and soaking in His presence. I had forgotten how incredible it was to just be silent... to just 'be'. I started speaking in my Heavenly Language again; and suddenly I was visualizing myself in the middle of a circle of several women.

God, what is this?

One thing Paula had taught me was to ask God for more information about the things you see — ask God what He wanted to show or tell you through the dreams/images that you see. I had never been good at it... but this picture was so clear. It felt real! One of the women in the circle was Paula, and another was Georgina. I saw them all lay hands on me and pray.

God, what are they praying for?

I kept asking questions and trying to focus on what was happening in the image, but I wasn't getting any revelation. I wasn't hearing a single answer.

~

As I approached Georgina, the Holy Spirit took control.

I can't believe I'm doing this!

"Hey. Can you come with me? I have to get you and a few others to pray for me."

Before arriving at church for the final session of the conference, God revealed to me what the image was.

I'm getting healed. God is going to heal me of my eating disorder.

While I was skeptical, and didn't fully believe I could be free, I decided to listen and gather all the ladies in the image. Maybe this act of obedience would propel me into a fresh season: a season of new beginnings and exciting opportunities. The other ladies in the picture didn't know about my eating disorder so I was scared to have them pray for me. Even though I knew them all, I would never have chosen them to pray for this. Thankfully, Paula was one of the ladies in the image... which was a huge reason why I willingly allowed the Holy Spirit to take lead. If I freaked out, Paula would be there.

"I'm getting a group of people to pray for me. I need you as well."

Paula followed as I found a somewhat secluded area at the front of the auditorium. My heart was beating rapidly. Not everyone I had asked had arrived yet, so I explained to Paula what I needed them to do. I can't tell them myself so Paula did the talking. I can't even look at everyone in the eyes as they encircled me. Bowing my head, all I could do was prepare my heart for whatever God was up to. The women placed their hands on me and I instantly got 'zapped' by the Holy Spirit. I knew whatever was about to take place would be indescribable... I could already feel it.

Paula started praying out loud first. She thanked God for creating me, and declared health and wholeness in my life. She interchanged between English and her Heavenly Language, constantly remaining in touch with God at all times. I closed my eyes, trying to block out every doubt I had about what God could do. The Spirit of God was so overwhelming, that I fell to the ground not long after the praying has commenced. I had no idea if anyone else had walked by and decided to join in praying. I couldn't even understand what was being said. I felt like I was floating. I started to cry and scream, covering my face with my arm in a vain attempt to hide my bawling. I felt like I did the night I first came to church, except this time there was a weird sensation in my stomach. It felt like a light entering me... a strobe light from Heaven - injecting goodness into my very core. I sensed Paula lying next to me, singing in her Heavenly Language. My Spirit leapt and I was touched afresh with a peace that calmed my entire body.

Thank You, God. Thank You, Lord.

I opened my eyes and realized I must have been on the floor for quite some time. There was hardly anyone left in the building! I stood up and hugged Paula.

"I'm so proud of you!"

I smiled, not really understanding what happened or why I felt so joyful. The energy charging through my body made it difficult to stand still. There was about eight people still roaming about, but I didn't care if they thought I was an idiot. I started jumping up and down, completely enthralled in God! For all He is... for all He does! I didn't want to say I was healed, just in case nothing actually happened. The truth is, I didn't know what it was like to live without an eating disorder. I didn't know what it was like to eat a meal without the overwhelming urge to throw it back up. I didn't know what it was like to look in a mirror and not hate everything you see. I didn't know a world without being ruled by calorie intake. I didn't know who I was without it.

God, teach me who I am...

As soon as I woke the next morning, I bolted to the bathroom. Despite the lingering doubt, I held on to hope that God healed me. Poised before the mirror, I looked myself in the eyes. My eyes were the only attribute I liked about myself but I had never really taken notice of how blue they were... especially this morning! I looked at my mouth. I had always hated my top lip, thinking it was too thin. I disliked my teeth and how crooked they were. I smiled and watched my cheeks puff out to accommodate the joy. I examined my nose where I had wanted to get plastic surgery since a little girl. I couldn't find a single flaw on my face! None at all! Not wanting to end my good luck by scanning my whole body, I decided to try some breakfast.

As I waited for the eggs to cook, I stood in awe of how different I felt. I put a slice of bread in the toaster and checked on my eggs. The biggest test would be keeping it down. Not purging was one thing, but feeling content to keep it down would be the judge. I put the toast on a plate and walked to the fridge. I grabbed a tub of butter and spread it across my toast. It was as though I was on autopilot. I reached for the pan with the scrambled eggs but froze midway.

I PUT BUTTER ON MY TOAST!!!

I PUT BUTTER!!!

BUTTER!!

ON MY TOAST!!!

BUTTER!!!

I hadn't willingly consumed butter since I was about ten years old. And here I was, about to chow down on scrambled eggs with BUTTERED toast!

I'm fine to look at myself in the mirror and now I'm eating butter?

I thought this was all too good to be true, so I decided to test God and see if He really did heal me. I sprinkled salt and pepper on top of my scrambled eggs. I had lived off such bland food for the past four years I couldn't even remember the last time I added extra flavoring to something I cooked. I sat at the table staring at my breakfast.

If I eat this entire meal, without guilt or purging... I will declare I'm healed.

I sat cross-legged in front of the therapist, flicking my shoelace. Paula was silent beside me... probably praying that today I would let my walls come down. Every inch of my body felt different. I could feel how each part of my body worked together, enabling me to do all I needed throughout the day. My stomach (that I once thought was too fat), was now seen as the 'holding ground' for the precious fuel that animated my wonderful adventures. My thighs which I once wanted to shred back to what I thought was thin, were now seen as strong, beautiful limbs — pulling me through even the darkest of days. My fingers, which I once thought were stumps of fat, were now seen as elegant instruments guiding my creative passions. In actual truth, I had the same body I always had, but everything was different. The mirror was no longer my enemy... now simply a reflection to alert me when I had food in my teeth. I hadn't weighed myself or obsessed over numbers in the two weeks since being prayed for. Instead, every morning I woke hungry and looked forward to making breakfast. I was eating lunch and tea... as well as snacks on the days I needed more energy.

"I was healed of my eating disorder at the conference."

The words flowed out before I could register what I was saying. It felt so natural.

I am healed.

I am healed.

"I AM HEALED!"

I looked over at Paula as a smile grew across her face. The room was quiet and I wondered if the therapist believed me. Mel would know how big a deal it was that I'd gone two weeks, eating every day and not throwing up. She would understand how huge it was for me to not break down every time I saw my reflection.

What if I kept it a secret too well and now I can talk about the years of being tortured by my own mind, nobody believes me? What if they don't consider me to have battled with an eating disorder because I wasn't thin enough?

"That's incredible!"

The therapist smiled and wrote something down on her note-pad. Paula was still beaming, which reminded me why I should stand tall as I declared the Goodness of God and what He has done.

"I got prayer from a few ladies... fell to the ground and began weeping... I guess I didn't really feel different immediately afterwards... but the next morning, everything had changed!"

I wondered how many more years I would have struggled if I hadn't listen to what I thought God was telling me. I wondered what would have happened if I didn't pay attention to the details of the images I saw.

"How do you feel about eating three meals a day now? Are you managing to keep it down?"

"I feel great! I don't even have the slightest urge to throw up. Food tastes too good!"

I chuckled at the immensity of this change. If God didn't save me when I tried to kill myself, I wouldn't have known this life. I wouldn't know what it was like to have buttered toast with my scrambled eggs. I wouldn't know what it was like to admire the way in which He created us and learn to truly love myself.

Is this why you saved me, God?

I began thinking about the times I bawled my eyes out because I hated the way I looked. I thought about all the tea and lunch dates I avoided because I was afraid to eat in front of others. I had begun dressing in baggy clothes around two years ago and I wondered if that would change now I was healed. I couldn't remember why I first started wearing loose clothing, but it soon became a way to hide my eating disorder. I had never been completely skin and bones but I had lost a lot of weight in a short period of time and I didn't want anyone to notice. I was excited for the day I could wear a T-shirt that didn't cover my butt. I was looking forward to the day I could wear a tank top and shorts in the summer. I tried to hold back tears as I remembered the last time I felt comfortable in my own skin. My mind flashed back to when I first decided I was fat. I was so young, yet so convinced the fat on my body made me disgusting. I was very young when I initially considered myself ugly compared to my friends. I was too young to be fixated on being skinny. I couldn't comprehend what might happen to me now. I was in a vulnerable place, but oddly enough, I wasn't afraid. I looked over at Paula who was probably still praying and praising God for this amazing miracle.

"It's a really awesome feeling."

I couldn't put into words how insane this was. I didn't know if the therapist would even understand. In the past, I hadn't been completely honest with how bad I was. Mel would be so happy. She might not understand right away how it was possible; nonetheless, she would be blown away! I fiddled with my shoelace, trying not to cry. I wasn't sure if I was emotional because I was finally processing how beautiful this moment was, or because I was scared of the things I still had to deal with. Now I didn't have to spend time in therapy discussing my poor body image and eating habits, there was more time to discuss the issues of my childhood and how they still preyed on me. I couldn't digress to my drinking issue anymore because I no longer felt any urge to drink my pain away. I couldn't talk about self-harm, because like the drinking, I had no compulsion to harm myself in that way. The eating disorder was the main coping mechanism I had been using to hide the pain of my childhood... and the self-harming and drinking attached itself to that.

The eating disorder was the home, and everything else I was doing to myself, were simply rooms in which I would hide out. No matter what room I was in (or what behavior I was engaging in), I was also still actively enmeshed in my eating disorder... regardless of what was going on around me. The eating disorder, although warping into different expressions over the years, was the one constant in my life. If I had a bad day, I could count on my eating disorder to give me the value and validation I craved. Counting calories made me happy. Skipping meals made me feel strong and in control. Purging granted me a sense of euphoria I didn't think I would be able to explain to someone who hasn't struggled with the grappling pull of an eating disorder. All of my patterns had been crafted from the beliefs that my eating disorder consoled and nurtured me. I had established my life in lies... lies that were so incredibly horrible they made me feel sick just thinking about them. I knew when I was healed, I would be able to finally get on the track to healing from my childhood... but I didn't feel ready. I thought dealing with it all now would make everything so much easier. I didn't want to go into a relationship still hurting from the hands that touched me. I didn't want to make things harder on my husband and be unsuccessful in breaking generational cycles. That is, I longed to be healed from my childhood, so my children wouldn't have to repeat the same mistakes and live the life I lived.

Becoming a Christian was a monumental step in the right direction to a better life (not only for myself, but my future husband and children), but claiming the title of a 'Christian' didn't magically solve all my problems. Yes, God works miracles... but I knew I had to step up to the plate as well. I knew He wanted to reveal so much to me through this journey. I knew I was going to grow as a person during the process of looking all my dark secrets in the eye. I knew He wanted to test me in my vulnerability. I was going to be stretched more than ever... but I knew it was all because He was teaching me something.

"What do you miss most about your family?"

I closed my eyes and took a deep breath.

God, I choose to trust You.

"I haven't really processed a single thing since I left home over a year ago. I think about them all a lot, but it's just really hard to remember things."

Every part of my body wanted to run out the door... to scream at the top of my lungs until the window shattered. I wanted Jesus to come back right this second so I wouldn't have to talk about this.

This is painful! God. I trust You but please don't make it so painful... Please.

Breathe. Breathe. Breathe. Breathe. Breathe.

"I don't know... I just miss a lot, I guess..."

God, I choose to trust You.

I sat in silence for what seemed like hours. I didn't know what to say or how to put words to my feelings. I was so thankful and blown away at the thought of being healed of my eating disorder and all God had done in my life since accepting Him into my heart a year ago... but I felt inadequate to deal with this.

I feel like I am at a crossroad between healing and staying where I am... and despite wanting to run down the path of healing, I want so badly to stay staring at the two. I don't know what to do.

You could hear a pin drop. The silence was oddly settling as I attempted to process the question and consider the possibility of that road to healing. I didn't think I would ever understand why God let such evil destroy my innocence, but I yearned to know what He was going to do with the destruction that continued to plague my heart.

God, I choose to trust You.

CHAPTER TWENTY FIVE

Tucking my knees up to my chest, I squished into a ball like a porcupine. My ears were ringing with the voices of the night — faceless people who haunted me when the sun lowered. I hadn't purged, restricted, cut or drowned my sorrows for two months. However, nightmares had taken their place. Every night I woke in feverish sweats, confused as to where I was. My mind was my worst enemy, convincing me I was in my childhood room. Most nights I would place my hand on the brick wall next to my bed to confirm I wasn't where I thought I was... that it was all just a dream. But tonight nothing was working. Scrunching into the fetal position was my last resort. Tears wet my face and my stomach ached from the silent sobbing.

I told God I trusted Him and I decided to commit wholeheartedly to walking the path of healing... but this entire process had been absolute torture! I had fallen back into the pattern of sleepless nights and during the daytime I was halted in my tracks by fear as flashbacks tormented my mind. I jumped at sudden movements and was more afraid than ever before. I had felt so free in my body since my healing, yet I remained entrapped by the nightmares that imposed upon my sleep. No matter what I tried to do, they wouldn't leave. Suppressed memories had been brought to the foreground, and I wasn't dealing with them well at all. I wanted somebody to understand — not just tell me they would be there for me as I continued to walk this journey. I wanted someone to tell me they understood what it was like to be terrified to fall asleep because your mind convinces you that you're back in the place you were abused. I wanted someone to understand what it was like to be so jumpy at every sudden movement. I wanted someone to understand the pain I was feeling during the healing season. I wanted someone to prove to me it was going to be worth it. I didn't want sympathy or more support networks; I just wanted someone to understand. I wanted a guarantee I could make it through this process of healing and not come out the other end more distraught than I already was.

God, I chose to trust you through this season? why are You making it so painful?

Tears continued to traverse down my face as I hugged my knees in tighter. I wanted to surrender everything to God, thinking that maybe being vulnerable with Him might help ease the pain. I opened the Pandora app on my iPhone to a worship station. I wanted to spend some time in His presence whilst the rest of the world slept. I was searching for answers and revelation to motivate me to keep walking this journey and not shut down. I yearned for a fresh touch from Heaven... to be reminded of His Goodness and Promises. The music that came on shuffle was a sure sign God wanted me to listen to Him. I cried more and more with each song that played. Every lyric was exactly what I needed to hear. My spirit was being stirred and revelation began pouring.

Good, Good Father by New Wine Worship
Fall Afresh by Bethel Music
Spirit Break Out by Soul Survivor
One Thing by Hillsong Worship
Hidden by United Pursuit
Cecie's Lullaby by Steffany Gretzinger

After *Cecie's Lullaby*, I turned off my phone and sat in silence, listening to the night critters outside my window rustling around in the darkness. My mind was now clear and the voices I usually heard every night were dimmed to a mere whisper. I wasn't sobbing anymore but tears were still pouring down my cheeks. I felt so at peace... embraced and protected by Him.

God, I'm so afraid. I'm afraid to be loved and to know what being loved really means. I'm afraid I can't break this cycle. Please, God, please give me the strength to continue walking this path of healing. I'm so afraid... so terribly afraid... of talking about what happened. I don't know what to do. I feel like such a wreck despite being on top of the world. I'm scared... really scared.

I sprawled across the floor with my arms wide open — ready to receive whatever God wanted to do. I was desperate for revelation. I knew my healing wasn't a random occurrence, and it was contributing toward the healing of my childhood. My eating disorder had been holding me back from moving forward. It was the harboring of secrets and suffering that stopped me from even making the smallest step towards a better life...always pulling me back, dragging me down and under... wrapping its chains around me tighter. Although I didn't feel ready to deal with my childhood (heck, I didn't think I'd ever be ready...), I knew it was time to unearth what I had submerged for so long. Now was the time, to be vulnerable and bask in His presence, as He poured out His Love over my terrorized and fragmented heart.

God, I choose to trust You!

~

I woke in the middle of the night for the third time that week... drenched in perspiration! It had become common for me to wake disoriented. It had also become a regular occurrence to lose myself completely in the darkness of the night. I bundled up, trying to rock myself back to sleep. My heart was racing as I heard the voices of those who weren't present. I begin shaking, at first I thought from a cool breeze flowing in the open window; but then I realized the window wasn't open and my heater was on. My mind was playing the cruelest cryptic games on me. I pulled my head down to my knees and used my arms to embrace my head in a headlock type position. I was no longer Stacey who had fled the danger. I was no longer Stacey who was healed, whole and walking courageously in the direction her heart so longed to flow. I was no longer Stacey — standing tall on the foundation of Her Father.

I was Stacey - with two long braids. I was Stacey who sang along to *High School Musical*. I was Stacey whose bedroom walls were covered in Zac Efron posters.I was Stacey who acted more like an adult than a fourth grader.

I could no longer feel the raised, pink scars that corrugated my stomach. Instead, I feel my pudgy youth - before self-hatred overpowered every inch of me. Instead of the shaved, short hair I currently sported, I could feel the thick fringe resting on my forehead. My heart beat faster and faster as I delved deeper into the illusion my mind was projecting. I sat up in bed, hoping everything would return to normal — that I would be anchored to reality — and feel like myself. Placing my feet on the floor, they rested on aged, scratchy carpet... not the soft carpet of my current house. My feet sprung back to the bed in record speed.

God, where are you?

I clambered out of bed and found my way to a corner to lie down. No matter how anxious or confused my thoughts, the floor was always my comfort — sure and steady. But it wasn't helping right now, because the corner of my room had changed. My desk — the one where I would hide as an eight-year-old to draw and write stories in my notebook — was in the corner. I was trapped in some obscure space...like an alternate reality.

I am here, but not really here.

I knew this wasn't real, but everything was screaming there was no escape... that I was stuck there.

God, I need you! Help!

I started sobbing again, not knowing why this was happening. Trying to focus on my breathing, I reminded myself it was going to be okay. Time seemed nonexistent as I huddled in the corner — the corner of the room I grew up in. My breathing began to slow down and I looked around. Everything was in the same position as when I was in primary school. Nothing was out of place.

God, what are you doing? I need You! Please! HELP!!!

I slowly stood, my legs trembling as I steadied myself. Standing in the room I grew up in, I examined my bod. My hands were chubby and I was wearing the jacket and shorts I wore almost every day when I was eight. Taking a deep breath, I walked toward the door. Only feet from the entrance, I heard someone walking up the hallway... toward my bedroom. I couldn't move!

This isn't real. You are fine. This isn't real. Breathe. You are fine.

Suddenly I experienced an intense feeling of peace. Moving toward the door again, I was no longer afraid to meet whoever was approaching. Again, I stopped still... but this time, from amazement.

Jesus.

I was no longer in the house where I grew up. Everything was black, as if my bedroom was the only room in this dark hole of confusion. Jesus walked straight past and stood adjacent from my bedroom door, looking ahead. I reached my hand out, but He was centered on what was happening in front of Him.

Jesus, I am here. I am here! Jesus!

I stepped closer, not knowing when I would wake from this messed up dream. Clothed in white, there was a luminous aura of light sparkling off Him. Tears ran down His cheeks — speechless at the sight before Him. I didn't want to look up. I didn't want to fix my eyes on what He was looking at. Even though everything was dark and I couldn't see anything else, I knew what was happening.

I am eight. I am eight years old!

Jesus, please stop it. STOP HIM!!

I wanted to scream. Why was He just standing there, weeping? I wanted to yell at Jesus! I wanted Him to put an end to what was happening right away!

Why aren't You stopping it? Right now! Jesus! Please! Stop it! Stop him!!!

Crying, I looked closer; searching desperately for something to pop out of the darkness. Suddenly, hands emerged. I was bawling... screaming! I registered those hands, remembered all the times they had touched me in ways they never should have. I wanted to be sick. The hands reached further towards me. They were about to grab me when I suddenly woke up... back in my own bed... my own room... back in the present.

I am Stacey, again. I am Stacey — with short, shaved hair. I am Stacey who is comforted and protected. I am Stacey who is healed and whole.

I wept until I was breathless. Jesus had stood right there... watching! He was watching and doing nothing! My entire world was being destroyed; and He just watched it! He stood there and allowed evil to invade my life and rob me of my purity. He stood there and watched it all happen.

God, what was that?

I sobbed at the overwhelming reality of what I had just experienced. Before that night, I had pondered the thought of Jesus being present during those times I was used in a way He never intended me to be. I had accepted that He saw every time I was violated, hurt and beaten. But never before had I seen and experienced His presence during those times. In all of my time considering the thought of Him being there, I had never felt so betrayed and livid... knowing He didn't stop the wickedness from destroying my innocence. I was gutted. I wanted to tell someone about what just happened, but I couldn't stand the thought of verbalizing it. To explain the dream, I would have to say out loud what those hands did to me... and I wasn't ready for that. I didn't want to remember.

GOD, I DON'T WANT TO REMEMBER!

My pillow was saturated from tears of frustration and malaise. I had been doing so wonderfully... with everything. Since my healing, I had grown tremendously. I perceived things in a different light, and my body was no longer my enemy.

Why is this happening? I feel as if all of the wonderful things I have achieved since my healing have now gone down the gurgler, even though I haven't actively done anything wrong. I feel defeated. I feel as though none of the good stuff matters any more. These nightmares have taken hold and are threatening to steer me off course. I needed to hold on to God's promises more than ever and continue trusting Him, even though nothing made sense anymore. If I wasn't going to let anyone in to this part of my world, then I knew I needed to be brave and vulnerable with the One who can restore.

God, it's time to get messy. I choose to trust You with everything, Lord...

CHAPTER TWENTY SIX

I was lost in His presence; arms wide open, all my attention focused on Him. It was as if no one else was around. The deeper I delved into His presence, the more I swayed. I could sense I was closer to the platform than when the worship first started, but I didn't care. I even didn't mind who could hear me crying out to God. I was so wrapped in His splendor nothing mattered. Completely overwhelmed with thankfulness, my mouth widened adoringly. I was pondering all the incredible things He had done for me, not only my healing, but the more discrete day-to-day, miracles.

Wow. Wow. Wow!!!! WOW!!!!!

Feeling like I could burst with all the joy coursing through my body, I wanted to stretch my arms wider... to smile bigger! Worship moments like this have become ones I treasure. During these times, God reveals more of who He is. He displays His vast, relentless Love for me. During these precious times of worship and admiration, my heart leaps at the thought of Him. I find myself growing in awe of The Father's heart - so incomprehensibly gracious and accepting. I dream where my life could go, where He wants me to go... extravagant, brave dreams. The worship was swelling through me, opening my heart to receive Heaven's pouring out, and I began to conjure up plans and present them to God. Over the past year, everything I ever dared to imagine for my life had fallen by the wayside. However, somehow I knew there were far greater things for me.

I was swaying faster, my arms dangling by my side, moving in opposite directions. I felt so free: full of unexplainable goodness. The worship leader was singing *'Good, Good, Father'* and I sobbed uncontrollably. I felt God's embrace with every word. Her voice sounded like an angel straight from Heaven; so beautiful — like nothing this world could produce. I placed my hand over my heart as the tears flowed.

"It's who I am... and I'm loved by You."

This is who I am, God! I am the girl who sways, jumps, dances and looks like an idiot as she worships. I am Your daughter, who pours everything out during worship. I am completely and utterly enthralled by You... given to You! This is who I am!

I opened my eyes, still burning with tears — in wonderment of His Majesty. The lights darted back and forth across the room, illuminating the faces of those lost in worship. This was the first time I was thankful, truly thankful for life since my suicide attempt. Not only because I was relieved to have had a good day or because I needed to be a 'good Christian' and thank God for what He had done, but I was thankful for life. I closed my eyes again and focused on His presence.

God, thank you! Thank you, thank you, thank YOU!

I was crying, but not just because of the song. I began crying — sobbing — at the thought of my future.

I should be dead! DEAD!!!

God didn't have to come in and save me. Not only the first time, when I became a Christian; but also the time I was seconds from death. He didn't have to do anything! But He did!

"You're a Good, Good Father..."

I couldn't even comprehend all the adventures and places God was going to take me.

I AM ALIVE!!! I have so much ahead of me. So much greatness to be a part of... and goodness to see. Wow!

I was crying at the thought of how close I was to not being here. I knew God didn't save me just so I could live an ordinary, mundane life. I didn't want to live an ordinary, mundane life.

God, use me! Lead me! Guide me... I choose to trust You!

I felt an immense sense of freedom flood over me, as though God was standing right behind me, holding me up... making me strong.

Oh Lord, I feel SO strong!

I felt as if I could walk out the church doors and conquer anything that came my way! My hands were on fire as I knelt in silence, letting God do whatever needed to be done. My veins felt like there was fire pulsating into them... blazing through my bloodstream! My hand tingled and jolted as a feeling of electricity buzzed over me. It was as if I was being recharged, ready to tackle the next season of life. The wear and tear of the last two years had left my bones fragile and heart weary. My eyes had been heavy and I felt burdened by what I had endured. However, the longer the worship lasted, the more I was restored.

More, Lord. Recharge me... I'm ready!

A verse from Psalms cleansed my heart as I repeated it to myself...

'God, You did everything You promised, and I'm thanking You with all my heart. You pulled me from the brink of death, my feet from the cliff-edge of doom. Now I stroll at leisure with God in the sunlit fields of life.'

(Psalms 56:12-13 MSG)

~

"Do you get lonely?"

I could hear the tone of my therapist's voice as I remembered a question she asked me several weeks ago. I couldn't stand to tell her the truth. In true 'Stacey style' I had avoided her question and downplayed how I really felt. I spent the majority of the sessions fiddling with my shoe and trying to count how many books lined the shelves spanning the entire length of the wall. I don't even know why she asked me... maybe it was an attempt to peel back layers and encourage me to be more vulnerable, but I didn't answer. So many things were running through my mind but the only thing I could conjure up was:

"Yeah, I guess. Not much, though."

Lonely?! Do I get lonely?! Oh please, you don't even know what it feels like to be lonely! You have a family to go home to. You have a job you love and most likely friends you've known for most of your life. You have formed years of memories with the people in your life and probably have traditions that make you happy and fill your life with great joy. Lonely? Lonely was what I was born in to! Lonely was what I felt as a kid, when I would play board games by myself. It's what I felt when I would cry myself to sleep, make my own school lunches, celebrate my 18th birthday drunk out of my mind.

Lonely was one of the first things I grew to believe was 'normal.' Lonely was the result of being lied to... about love. Lonely forced its way into my bones and plagued my life.

Do I get lonely?
Lonely...
Isolated?
Friendless?
Abandoned?
Unloved?
Outcast?
Sad?
Depressed?
Rejected?
Alone?
"Do you get lonely?"

You don't know what it feels like to be lonely until you realize there isn't a single person who knows what it's like to go through what you've been through. When there isn't anyone who can understand the nightmares, the flashbacks, the struggle of reminding yourself every day it's over. You don't know what lonely means until you're left alone and forced to work out life. When you have to start being an adult sooner than a child should be.

Lonely? Do I get lonely?! No. I don't *get* lonely...I *AM* lonely.

Life would be so much easier if I said what was really on my mind. If I just swallowed my pride for once and allowed myself to be transparent, I would move much faster through the recovery process! I guess I was scared to be thrown into a psych ward again, even though I wasn't suicidal anymore. Heck, I loved life. I really did. But I had no idea how therapists worked and what their protocol for sending clients to the looney bin was. Maybe I was over-thinking everything, but I sure didn't want to risk my chances. I'd prefer to dilute everything and take twice as long to fully heal.

"Do you get lonely?"

"Do you get lonely?"

"Do you get lonely?"

I couldn't shake the question out of my head. I was back at the beach, looking out to the ocean, focused on my breathing. The sun was close to setting, and like usual, the entire stretch of the beach was deserted. I was at a crucial place in life. It was like I was standing at a physical, mental, and spiritual crossroad. There were so many turns I could choose. I could take the path to God and continue walking with Him through vulnerability and restoration. This would eventually lead me to a greater sense of His love and peace, and a deeper understanding of my identity in Christ. I knew this was the path I needed to take and it certainly

was the path I wanted to take. But there was also another path...
one I felt I could easily begin to walk without even noticing. It
was the path of closed doors and secrets. Where honesty is never
explored and healing becomes elusive... Where spending time
with God would be a chore and the chaotic day-to-day would
sweep me up and carry me out to a sea in which I couldn't stay
afloat. God has given us a free will. It was time for me to honor
this gift, and make the right choice with my heart — with my
life.

Do you get lonely?

Do you get lonely?

Do you get lonely?

I took several deep breaths... inviting the Holy Spirit to invade my heart. I allowed my mind to settle and my ears to become fine-tuned to the Whispers of Heaven.

"God, I don't want to be lonely anymore."

I closed my eyes and began speaking out loud. It was almost
dark, so nobody would be coming on to the beach.

"God, I don't want to be lonely. I don't want to be lonely
anymore."

Consumed with hot Holy Spirit tingles, I began crying.
I could sit on this beach for hours... listening to the truth He
wanted to wash over me. I could sit for days, forgetting about

every worry and allow His precious love to permeate me... to remind me who I really was.

"I know I am loved and wanted by You, Lord. And you will never forsake or abandon me. But..."

I took a deep breath, reminding myself it was okay to get messy with Him.

"Please make me feel all those things deep within my soul. Make me feel it in my bones... where loneliness has hollowed me out and made a home. God, I want to not just feel it... but I want to *know* it."

As the darkness cloaked my silhouette, I began humming *'Good Good, Father.'* I lay back on the sand — arms outstretched — my default position when I was getting serious with God.

"Strengthen me, Lord. Let me get messy... messier than I've ever been. I'm ready. I'm so ready, God."

"Don't be afraid, for I am with you.

Don't be discouraged, for I am your God.

I will strengthen you and help you.

I will hold you up with my victorious right hand."
(Isaiah 41:10 NLT)

CHAPTER TWENTY SEVEN

For the first time in my life I felt lighter on my feet... strong and fresh... like the morning after being healed of my eating disorder. Except this time was more intense... as if my face could split in two from grinning. My life was flashing before my eyes as I remembered all the incredible things God had done in my life over the past eighteen months. Every part of me knew I shouldn't be alive. Every inch of my body knew I should be a cripple or still caught in a sinful, addiction-riddled, fear-stricken life. Fixated on the sky, my feet were walking a familiar route. I was remembering that time in hospital, gazing into the bluest sky I had ever seen... the moment I had prayed for the first time. I had been given more chances than I deserved. I chuckled as I remembered every stereotype I believed about Christians. How I never thought I would become a crazy Christian — not in my wildest dreams! Yet here I was... obsessed with Jesus. A desire was rising from deep within — to preach the Gospel and help others caught in the life I once lived.

Oh Lord, You are SO Good!

Turning the corner, I pointed toward the street I lived in after I left the shelter. I had sworn I would never return to this place, but it wasn't my own mind that decided to come here! With each step, I realized some great revelation was about to take place. As I walked up the hill towards the street, it was apparent I was a lot healthier than the last time I took this route. I would always labor the slight incline, hauling a backpack full of binge food I bought from the local corner store and end up fatigued from skipping meals or purging. Additionally, while walking this route, I would be mulling over my intentions to spend the next couple of hours sprawled out over the bathroom floor. This time, my face brightened as I approached the street, knowing something beautiful was about to occur.

An empty vodka bottle littered the side of the road — something I never saw when I lived there. I would usually see XXX Gold or James Bought cans... even the occasional empty goon bag... but never vodka! As I closed in on the street I started speaking in tongues. My heart was beating at a normal speed, something that would never happen on my 'binge route' back home. Every step uphill felt comfortable — my breathing was easy, rhythmic. Still early, there was hardly anyone in the streets. I had never been afraid of my neighbors, however I was scared to walk this street alone. It's weird how nothing seems to phase you when you're in a constant state of darkness. I drew in a deep breath as I walked by the houses that were once my neighbors. I was praying for every household in the street, something I attempted to do before I moved out but never with faith attached. I knew if I was able to have my life transformed, nothing was impossible for these people who still call this street their home.

Stopping in front of my old house, memories came rushing through my mind. All those nights lying on the lounge room floor. The days I couldn't leave my bed because depression and anxiety restrained me. The countless hours crying in the kitchen as I debated whether or not to eat. The stretches of time sprawled out across the bathroom floor. Those moments I had to hold myself back from walking out the door and never coming back. It seemed strange reflecting on it all... knowing that not too long ago it was my reality.

Thank You, God. Thank You!

If you stand in a certain place on this street and look between the rooftops, you can see straight down to the ocean. The morning sun reflected elegantly off the water and my heart mirrored its warmth and comfort. I couldn't believe that all the time I lived in this neighborhood I had never taken advantage of the view and imbibed its serenity. I continued down the street, still praying and speaking in tongues. An empowering assurance emboldened my every step. Reaching the end of the street I turned around and surveyed the rows of houses lining each side... the crooked mailboxes perched at every driveway. Mercifully, this was not where my story finished. Overflowing with thankfulness, I glowed, knowing my life was above and beyond what it had been. That street will forever have a special place in my heart. It is where I had my firsts: my first encounter with the Holy Spirit, the first home I lived in by myself, the first time I stayed awake for 72 hours straight, my first read of a Bible. It will forever be the street where my mind will wander to 'where it all started'.

Thank You God, for saving me.

'You are blessed when you're at the end of your rope.

With less of you there is more of God and His Rule.

You're blessed when you feel you've lost what is most dear to you.

Only then can you be embraced by the One most dear to you.'

(Matthew 5:3-4 MSG)

SOZO
Saved. Healed. Whole.

Right now, as I write this, I am buzzing with anticipation at the possibilities of all that could happen in my life. I am overwhelmed at God's Goodness and the ways in which He continues to bless and sustain me. I think back to the time where I was seconds away from taking my own life and I can't help but cry... although not entirely from sadness. Rather, I cry with a heart full of thankfulness. The lessons I have learnt since reaching such a low point have imbued me with a strength that astounds me every day. Living in such a dark place provoked me to press in closer to my Father. The depth of the darkness I was in, allowed His Light to shine brighter than most people may ever see. I have grown in leaps and bounds as I continue to put my trust in God. It is a commitment I make every morning, as well as constantly throughout the day. Life is great, spectacular if you may, but it certainly has its hardships and disappointments. Regardless of how deep our faith may be or how strong our relationship with God, life is still going to happen! The good and the bad and our faith is tested. Challenges threaten to knock us down and steer us off the path we're walking with the Lord.

I am learning to embrace every season of life and no matter my circumstances, to praise God with all I have - in all of my ways — for all of my days.

ED is no longer around, but loving and accepting all that still remains is a challenge. It is a challenge that I am getting better at with each day. Today, I eat at restaurants! With friends... and by myself! I am learning to genuinely like what I see when I look in the mirror. I feel so secure and comfortable in my own skin – something which I never thought I could say, let alone feel! I stand with my arms wide open, occasionally clenching my heart as I am reminded of the life I was saved from. Free from all the chains that held me captive, tears stream down my cheek as I rest in a peace in all that I am – and all that I am growing up to be. Some mornings, the realization of the life God saved me from brings me to my knees and I sob as I remember the darkness He raised me from... and as I think upon the light He is now helping me walk in.

I also get emotional at things I couldn't previously stand the thought of... you know, simple routine things like eating three meals a day and going back for seconds. After all, sometimes food is just too good to eat only one time! I catch myself every now and then being amazed by how natural my new life has become. It brings such delight, to recognize that I automatically replace lies with HIS truths.

I am blown away at the thought of how well my body continues to serve me. I am fascinated by all the ways my body is going to do remarkable things as I continue to grow. No longer fixated on the scales, calorie intake or how I look; instead, I am focused on my inner self. When I pass by mirrors I smile, because it's just a reflection of my physical person... not who I really am. I have a level of self-control and self-awareness that catches me off guard and makes me realize more and more the magnitude of the Father's Love.

Micah 7:7 is a verse that I hold close to my heart and reflect over on a regular basis. It has stayed with me since God saved me from taking my own life... and I believe it will forever serve as a reminder of His Goodness and promises.

'But me, I'm not giving up.

I'm sticking around to see what God will do.

I'm waiting for God to make things right.

I'm counting on God to listen to me.'

(MSG version)

The New Living Translation version reads...

'As for me, I look to the Lord for help.

I wait confidently for God to save me

and my God will certainly hear me.'

I think of this as a 'life verse.' Although there are many scriptures in the Bible which I hold on to for daily wisdom and guidance, Micah 7:7 is one I want my character to be built upon. I want to be someone who doesn't give up despite what may be happening around me. Micah 7:7 is such a beautiful verse because it is full of faith.

"...I'm waiting for God to make things right..." I can get impatient when waiting, but I've learned God's timing is perfect and

sometimes the waiting period provides great growth and beautiful revelation.

"... my God will certainly hear me." For me, it's daunting to trust someone so much to believe they will 'certainly' hear me. No matter how softly I may whisper (or how loud I may roar), I am most certain my God will hear me!

Anxiety still threatens to hold me captive from time to time, and to be honest, sometimes I don't fight as hard as I know I should. I'm learning to let go and run to God in those moments. I'm learning the importance of being vulnerable. I'm allowing myself to cry my tears and voice my frustrations. I am aware the journey to healing is arduous and long. To be honest, I'm still in the earlier stages. I'm not quite sure when I will reach the end, or even if it will ever be complete this side of Heaven. But the strength I am gaining as I walk this path *with God* is incredibly powerful and awe-inspiring. I have chosen to adopt a warrior mentality instead of a victim mentality. I invite His truth to wash me afresh and my mind to be transformed. I don't want to be held back by my past or stunted because of what has happened to me. I choose to walk boldly in the direction my heart longs to be. No matter what happens, I know I am loved and I am a warrior who gives everything I have.

There is so much confidence that is yet to come – confidence that will break guilt and shame and leave me with a new style. Confidence that will propel me to new heights and leave all the old behind. This confidence isn't something that feels far away, or something that 'maybe one day' might appear. It is a confidence that is slowly building within... just waiting to burst and manifest into every area that is currently lacking.

In the quiet times, I find myself rejoicing at the absence of that ache in my heart. That dark cloud of depression no longer engulfs me and I can dance with freedom. Truth and positivity have found their home in me. Self-hatred has to flee. I move freely in the Spirit — shooting arrows of praise to the High Heavens, declaring the Goodness of the One Who has won my heart. The more I think about the Love of God, the more I am undone... the more my heart bursts with adoration for all He is. If I could, I would sit for endless days, just being totally wrecked, consumed by the thought of His devotion and faithfulness.

Maybe we all need to take time to do this more often. It has offered some of the most beautiful revelations that have pulled me over hurdles as I continue to walk the path of restoration. I have realized I'm not quite sure yet who I am. In my efforts to help myself, I had gathered my broken pieces, trying to hold them tentatively together, but I have come to understand I was only hurting myself. Through trial and error, being still in His presence and choosing to trust Him — with everything... I'm slowly learning the truth of who I am. My identity is being shaped by Biblical truths, molding me into the child He created me to be all along.

I will continue to dance and laugh and learn to embrace the skin that I am in, scars and all the imperfections that may be! I will continue to look on the bright side and remind myself of the victorious warrior that now stares back at me in the mirror. I choose not to be a victim, but an overcomer. A warrior. I choose to be all that I was called to be by the One Who created me. I'm not sorry for my mess, my tears, my awkwardness... for anything. From all of the broken pieces, something incredibly special is being created.

I am learning I am deeply loved by the King... a daughter of the Most High. I am worthy, forgiven, saved, and embraced. I am thought of — and adored. I am protected and I have such a Good, Good Father.

I am S.J Rye... and I am blessed in the darkness.

Celebrate with me. Celebrate this life that was headed down a dead beat, grave ending track. A life that now has a future – a future so big and wonderful that the possibilities of what could happen make me so excited! Celebrate the triumphs – the small victories and new days. Stand with me as I dance and laugh and embrace this gorgeous, beautiful, awe-inspiring life that is before us.

I could write an entire book thanking every single person that deserves praise. The following people have either helped by contributing in a big way, or with simple gestures that went a long way. I am forever grateful to you all! Along with those listed, I would like to thank every single person who purchased and read my book. I am so happy and honored you thought my story was not only worthy of your money, but also your time! I pray *Blessed in the Darkness* has enriched you and you are able to walk away with something you didn't have before reading. From the bottom of my heart, thank you!

JILL JAMESON

Mama Jill, wow! I love you so, so much!!! Thank you for showing me what it's like to be loved and a part of a family. Thank you for being so caring and non-judgmental... even when I say and do the most ridiculous things! Thank you for pushing me to do and be the best I can possibly be. Thank you for always saying it like it is and knowing how to make me laugh. I appreciate the influence you have in my life and for all the ways you care for me. I will forever be grateful for the wisdom you continue to impart. Thank you for being so patient with me and the role model I always needed.

PAULA PROCTOR

No matter how well God may have blessed me with words, it is impossible to think of the right ones when it comes to saying how thankful I am for you! Thank you for consistently walking with me during some of the darkest days and not giving up. Thank you for teaching me valuable lessons that have helped in my spiritual journey as well as life in general. Thank you for teaching me it's okay to cry. Thank you for teaching me how to keep a promise and leading by example. So much love for you!

KEN OVERTON

Thank you for your generosity and willingness to believe in a girl who was crazy enough to believe in a God dream. This wouldn't be possible without you. Thank you so much!

HANNAH HARRINGTON

Thank you for being such an incredible friend. Thank you for not letting distance or any stupid decisions get in the way of our friendship. Thank you for letting me vent and making me laugh when nothing else can. I cannot wait to go on many more wild adventures and create more memories. Thank you for being YOU! I feel so blessed to have you in my life. LYLATS!

KRISTEN O'KEEFE, RACHEL BROWN, MONICA CORBETT, & TONYA FORWARD

Thank you for being the very first people to back me on this wild ride. Thank you for being incredible women of God who are extravagantly generous with goodness and love.

MEGHAN SHEARER

Thank you for eating burgers with me and knowing what good coffee is. Thank you for going on adventures with me and for just being a fun friend to have in life! Your humor and sincerity fill my heart with so much love.

MEL

Thank you for your wisdom and time. Thank you for showing me there's so much in me that the world needs.

HANNAH KING

Girl!!! Thank you for your wisdom, patience, silence, and your heart that is so full of the Fathers Love. I appreciate the way you carry yourself in every situation... it's inspiring! Thank you for all you do for me and for sharing my humor. Your gift of singing has wrecked me so many times and taken me in to countless intimate moments with God — helping me to write this book. Thank you for being such a great friend through every season.

JUSTIN BROWNE

Thanks for all the talks around the pool table! You are such a unique person... please never change. Keep being who you are... the hilarious, random bloke we all know and love. Thanks for being one of the first people to understand what it's like to be such a lost kid and for constantly encouraging me throughout my journey.

DYLAN PROCTOR & JAMES BREWER

Your talent astounds me! Thank you for helping me make this all look pretty and capturing what my hands couldn't create. Also, thank you for being two terrific blokes who carry Jesus' Love so incredibly well.

JENNIFER EMMERTON

Your wisdom and expertise astound me! Thank you so much for taking on this little baby and helping me in the final stages. You are tremendous!

AMANDA BUTEL

Thank you for being my wordsmith and go-to-lady! Your wisdom and endless encouragement is the reason this all happened. Thank you for being such a remarkable daughter of The King! I am in awe of the Love that oozes out of you. Thank you so much... for everything!

Loved *Blessed in the Darkness?* Want to share a story with S.J or book her to speak at an event? Send her an email at:

contact@sjrye.com

Or follow S.J on her social media accounts:

Facebook.com/thesjrye

Instagram: @thesjrye

www.ingramcontent.com/pod-product-compliance
Lightning Source LLC
Chambersburg PA
CBHW032013050726
47590CB00006B/2152